Alone
Within the Pack

by Sandra Lynch-Bakken

For Dale,
my life mate and best friend,
whose love and support helped turn a dream into a reality.

For my parents,
who filled my childhood with wonderful camping trips.

And for my daughter Amanda,
who brings beauty into the world just by being herself.

Ecopress
An Imprint of Finney Company

Alone Within the Pack
Copyright © Sandra Lynch-Bakken, 2008

Ecopress
An Imprint of Finney Company
8075 215th Street West
Lakeville, Minnesota 55044
www.finneyco.com
www.ecopress.com

ISBN 10: 1-893272-11-7
ISBN 13: 978-1-893272-11-8

Photography by Sandra Lynch-Bakken
and Dale Bakken
Designed by Angela Wix
Edited by Lindsey Cunneen

Printed in the United States of America
1 3 5 7 9 10 8 6 4 2

Contents

Introduction
1

Chapter 1: *Wolf Woods*
9

Chapter 2: *The Heritage Pack*
17

Chapter 3: *Finding Her Place*
25

Chapter 4: *The Family Shadow*
39

Chapter 5: *Puppy Love*
49

Chapter 6: *Wolves Are Wild, Dogs Are Domestic*
65

Chapter 7: *Solo's Reign*
73

Chapter 8: *The Pack's Fury*
83

Chapter 9: *The Darkness Returns*
95

Chapter 10: *The Pack Divides*
115

Epilogue
119

Introduction

It was an April day like most others that month—"typical" is how the locals described it. Nothing set it apart. The snowfall of 1993 had been heavy but would not break any records. Besides, snow was a part of life in the Bitterroot Mountain Range of Montana. Nevertheless, it did seem to come early and did not let up until April.

In defiance of winter's grasp, spring emerged and the signs were everywhere. A pine grosbeak balanced gracefully on a snowberry bush. A groggy hoary marmot poked his head from his cozy winter crevice to scan the skies for anything that might regard him as lunch. On a south-facing hillside of the Flathead Valley, in a frost-free underground refuge called a hibernaculum, hundreds of red-sided garter snakes began to stir. Each reptile glided effortlessly over the others in search of the warmth of the cave opening and a long-awaited meal.

On this spring day, a tawny wolf pup whimpered when she became separated from the heat of her mother's body. Unable to regulate her own body temperature, she crawled back toward the warm mass of fur and vied with her littermates to reach her mother's teat. Strong intuition, along with her mother's nudging, guided her to that fattening "first milk." Being blind and the runt of the litter, reaching that lifeline was not so easy, but her fortitude kept her alive during those first critical hours.

For the next two years, Shilo's life was far from ideal. Born into captivity at the Triple D Ranch in Kalispell, Montana, to meet the growing wolf craze, she was housed alone in a 6' by 12' dog kennel. She was kept separated from other wolves, teased constantly by hearing and seeing her own kind, and yet denied an innately desired life with a pack. She was often seen hoarding food. Some biologists believe this act can represent a mode of displacement behavior, an activity that distracts the wolf from a stressful situation.

Shilo, born April 1993. Shown here at Triple D Ranch, she was very thin and her fur was sparse and ragged.

The wolves' pens in Kalispell, Montana.

Shilo's parents were allowed to breed, to create another litter of captive wolves that would generate revenue through their sale or use as subjects for wildlife photographers. However, Shilo's nervousness made her a poor camera model, so she became dispensable. No longer wanted or needed, she was a financial burden rather than a profit generator. Her owner did not hesitate to advertise in the *Animal Finder's Guide* publication: "Purebred Alaskan gray wolf FREE to good home."

One might think that a captive wolf would be guaranteed a life without challenges—that since food, shelter, companionship, and medical treatment are provided, life-and-death struggles belong exclusively to wild wolves. But Shilo's life would disprove this rosy theory. She would fight to find her place.

Meanwhile, hundreds of miles south of Shilo's home, wolf biologists in Wyoming were rejoicing. *Canis lupus*, the gray wolf, had burst onto the global stage in the winter of 1995. Prior to that year, if you weren't a wolf enthusiast who purposefully sought out news of wolves, the word "wolf" tended to be a history lesson on humanity's dark and tumultuous relationship with the predator. "Wolf" was a reminder of individuals and organizations banning together to attempt to eradicate the species from the face of the earth.

The Yellowstone Wolf Reintroduction Program produced a surprisingly intense interest in wolves across North America. The wolf fervor gained such momentum that zoos in both Canada and the United States recognized the ecological significance of displaying these animals and souvenir shops throughout the Northwest carried all types of wolf relics.

Unlike some conservation programs that seemed implemented purely for consumptive uses (like Ducks Unlimited and Pheasants Forever), the wolf release campaign gained notoriety based solely on correcting an imbalance in the ecosystem. By releasing gray wolves back into their former range as primary predators, the hope was that their presence would convert the land to its previous, healthier state.

In the early weeks of 1995, fourteen gray wolves were airlifted from Alberta, Canada, to the northern region of Yellowstone National Park in Lamar Valley, Wyoming. Seventeen more Canadian wolves would make the same trip the following year. These animals had been previously tracked, snared, collared, and released back to the Rock Lake, Alberta, area in 1994. On the day the project team was ready to

Wolves in their kennels at Triple D Ranch.

relocate those wolves to Yellowstone, the temperature was minus thirty as they hung out the open door of the helicopter and darted the collared wolves below.

Three one-acre pens had been constructed earlier to each hold one family group. The intent was to keep pack members together and reduce their stress levels, as well as persuade the families to stay together. Once the gates were opened in Yellowstone, the wolves would hopefully not rush off in different directions or try to head back to Canada.

All of these wolves were considered guinea pigs for the reintroduction program. Several would lose their lives for this scientific undertaking, but the howls of those that survived would echo throughout the valley and reinvigorate the ideals of environmental conservation.

The issue was hotly debated between those who were in favor of wolves in the park and those who were against. There seemed to be no in-between.

Organizations such as Defenders of Wildlife financially compensated local ranchers for legitimate livestock deaths from wolves, but many of the ranchers believed wolves should be killed. They believed there was no room for both, and if given a choice, they would banish wolves in a heartbeat. Cattle, after all, were their livelihood.

Early in the eradication era, estimates of wolf numbers in the Yellowstone region exceeded 35,000. Eradication policy was not based solely on the belief that wolves were vermin and needed to be eliminated, but also on the fur market and how it shifted from beaver pelts to hides of elk, deer, bison, and wolves. Between 1860 and 1885 the new occupation of "wolfing" took hold. In the 1870s hundreds of thousands of bison were slaughtered, many settlers moved west, and cattlemen brought tens of thousands of livestock from Texas, Colorado, Kansas, and Nebraska to Montana's and Wyoming's prairies. As a result, the wolves' prey dwindled. The settlers—trappers, miners, homesteaders, and steamboat workers—needed meat and soon shifted their focus from bison to deer, elk, moose, antelope, and bighorn sheep, depleting those food sources as well. Plummeting numbers of prey turned sportsmen militant with regards to predator control. They were not about to share what was left of the prey base with wolves, and thus the massive wolf extermination began.

Dens were dynamited; animals were burned alive; some had their eyes seared with hot irons or their mouths wired shut and then were released to ultimately starve to death. Certain "wolfers," as they came to be called, found a devastatingly effective method of killing wolves. They would kill a buffalo every three or four miles and inject strychnine into the tongue, flanks, and entrails of the animal. Wolves unknowingly ate the tainted buffaloes and died nearby. Dozens of wolves were often found dead near the poisoned buffalo carcass.

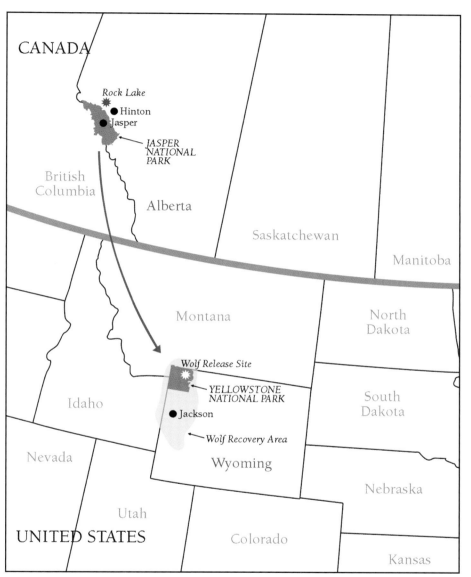

CANADA

Rock Lake
● Hinton
● Jasper
← JASPER
NATIONAL
PARK

British
Columbia

Alberta

Saskatchewan

Manitoba

Montana

North
Dakota

Wolf Release Site
← YELLOWSTONE
NATIONAL PARK

Idaho

South
Dakota

● Jackson

Nevada

← Wolf Recovery Area

Wyoming

Nebraska

Utah

UNITED STATES

Colorado

Kansas

In 1995, fourteen wolves were relocated from an area east of Jasper National Park in Alberta, Canada, to Yellowstone National Park in Wyoming.

The Montana Veterinary Service helped by infecting wolves with sarcoptic mange—in which female mites burrow under the skin to lay their eggs—causing an epidemic of the debilitating parasitic skin disease. But ranchers wanted additional help to wipe out this enemy. They got the Montana legislature to pass the first bounty law in 1883, which awarded hunters one dollar for every wolf pelt presented to either a justice of the peace or a probate judge. Once this was done the hunter then sold the pelt to fur buyers. This was incredible incentive, so much so that 5,450 wolves were killed in the first year after the bounty act became law.

At the end of the nineteenth century, even conservationist William Hornaday saw wolves as despicable, mean, and treacherous. Yet wolves demonstrated intellect and cunning by being wary of the poisoned carcasses purposefully left behind by hunters. They became adept at avoiding traps and some would travel more than fifty miles to escape a hunting party. However, in the end, through the joint efforts of the U.S. Biological Survey and the National Park Service, wolves were eradicated from 95 percent of their North American range.

But wolves are an intrinsic part of nature's web, so conservationists in the 1990s became convinced that wild spaces would be healthier with their presence. The wolf's incredible resourcefulness encouraged advocates to attempt to restore wolves back to the wild. Of course, some park neighbors were quite happy with the wolf's absence from the Great Plains since 1930. But even though their attitudes remained unaltered as the Yellowstone project began, wolf supporters were confident that the restoration would succeed.

Far too often we see one side to humankind—the vile side. It is confirmed every day in the news, but now and then a magical moment revives our faith in each other. That is exactly what the world witnessed on that frigid March day in 1995 when the gates to the Rose Creek pens were finally opened. Alpha male Number 10, the sole member of his pack to have been captured in Canada, was the first to break from the pen, becoming the first wolf to journey the wilds of Yellowstone in six decades.

A month later he became the father of eight pups. He had mated with female Number 9, who had shared his acclimation pen during the winter months, to produce a new generation of wild wolves. But the celebration was cut short with a painful reminder of humanity's uneasy relationship with wolves. Number 10 was shot and killed on April 23rd by a man who claimed he thought it was a wild dog. Wolf advocates across the country were stung with sadness, and as for me, as a Canadian, I was angry. It seemed as though we were sacrificing these unsuspecting wolves, lining them up to be slaughtered. I condemned the project but later recanted when I learned that Canada endorses annual wolf hunts in numerous provinces, with no limit on the number of wolves taken in many of those regions. Suddenly I was less than a proud Canadian.

Whether American or Canadian, if you were a wolf supporter, Number 10's death was a sorrowful day. He would never teach his pups how to survive this harsh, cruel world. His death left his mate a single parent. How would she survive? How would she be able to raise her pups alone?

Hateful attitudes still exist; it is difficult for some to accept living with a predator perceived as a food competitor for both domestic and wild ungulates. Yet, with the wolf's strong supporters from the scientific and non-ranching worlds, sheer numbers tip the scales in favor of preservation. However, when two predators collide in the same space, history suggests which one will prevail—the one with the dirtier tricks. Humans are quick to wipe out a species perceived as threatening, even if it means destroying an ecosystem.

The mid-nineteenth century marked a change in our relationship with the planet and its creatures. What was once symbiotic began to turn parasitic, and the evidence came in the form of a letter from Chief Seattle to President Franklin Pierce. He wrote, "Where is the eagle? Gone. Where is the buffalo? Gone. The white man takes from the land whatever he needs. The earth is not his brother but his enemy and when he has conquered it he moves on. Continue to contaminate your bed and you will one night suffocate in your own waste."

Centuries later, humans continue to take from the planet at a gluttonous rate, whereas the wolf and raven, throughout time, have nurtured their mutually beneficial relationship. The raven signals potential prey to the wolf and the wolf in turn allows the raven to feed at the kill. We would do well to learn a few things from animals.

Our wildlife achievements are often tainted by our barbaric exploits. Perhaps one day the beauty and dignity of wolves will be felt by all and the idea of destroying such a splendid creature will be unthinkable.

Regardless of some people's objections and intolerance, the Yellowstone wolves continue to make their mark in the wilderness. Against many odds they roam their wild land and, for now, are allowed to stay. More wolf pups are born in and around the park, their numbers surpassing 300. This is good news to many, foul news to some. The debate, fueled by hate, respect, misconceptions, and adoration, is ongoing.

By the time the winter of 1995 ended, wolves had become a high profile animal, one that carried a powerful conservation message. Zoos and other captive facilities knew if they were to keep pace with the growing environmental movement and fulfill their mission statements of conservation through education, they needed to house gray wolves. The *Canis lupus* band wagon was about to get crowded.

Facilities of all sizes throughout North America, both accredited and non-accredited, combed private breeders, sanctuaries, and other zoological parks for surplus wolves—adults, juveniles, or pups, it did not matter. This was the beginning of a new, and hopefully better, life for these wolves, including Shilo. 🐾

Chapter 1

Wolf Woods

The author's parents, Ron and Helen Lynch, at the Heritage Zoo sign.

Summer's heat began to surrender to fall's brisk embrace. The Yellowstone wolf saga, although still fresh on everyone's mind, took a momentary backseat for those of us who worked at Heritage Zoo. In a matter of days, my husband Dale and I would drive to Montana to pick up four captive gray wolves and bring them back to the zoo. Taxonomists—biologists who classify plants and animals into species, subspecies, and other categories—recognize five subspecies of gray wolves in North America. The wolves coming to our zoo were of the subspecies *Canis lupus occidentalis*.

Heritage Zoo logo and front entrance.

Heritage Zoo in Grand Island, Nebraska, created Wolf Woods for four wolves that would come from Triple D Ranch in Kalispell, Montana.

Our six-acre Heritage Zoo was nestled in the middle of the city of Grand Island, Nebraska. Its nine staff members were a strange cast of characters. In some ways, we mirrored a wolf pack. Dale, the director of the zoo, was the undisputed alpha. Joel, the maintenance supervisor, and Tom, the herpetologist, jostled for beta position. One of the feline keepers was the definite omega. At times she was ridiculed by other keepers for petty reasons. She was the least physically fit of all the keepers and when there was a truck full of hay or meat to be unloaded, she usually made herself scarce. Also, her blonde, gelled hairdo seemed overdone compared to the tightly tied ponytails of the other women.

As for the rest of the zoo staff, we were subordinates with no fixed rank, but like a wolf pack we bonded together with a single focus—to give the best possible care to our animal family.

For weeks the entire staff worked tirelessly to put the finishing touches on the new exhibit, Wolf Woods. We dragged in dead tree limbs, dumped buckets of earth on top of the man-made den to hide it from the visitor's view, and hauled in more dirt to form a nine-foot lookout mound, which would later be known as Solo's Summit. Everyone was silly with excitement for the wolves' approaching arrival.

We understood what an honor it was to have these carnivores become part of our zoo collection. Small facilities tend to have to work harder to succeed, and the teamwork was evident with the opening of the new exhibit. The hierarchy of responsibility and duty quickly faded when something needed repairs or an exhibit needed building. Everyone picked up shovels to dig dens, slipped on leather gloves to string cage wire, swung hammers to build night houses, and dragged dead logs and rolled boulders to enhance the habitat. Providing the wolves with a natural and stimulating environment was important to us all. We did not have a million-dollar budget, but that did not stop us from creating a great home for our newest charges.

Dee, the Education and Marketing Coordinator, was sitting at her desk and watching the naked mole rats chisel their way through the corncob bedding to create a labyrinth inside their terrarium when the office phone rang. The quiet of the September morning was pierced.

"All radio units, this is Zoo Base. Dale just called. He and Sandra will be here by supper time with the wolves," Dee cheerfully announced. "Plus, there's fresh banana bread up here whenever you get a chance."

A grin crossed her pretty face as she placed the radio back in its cradle. Dee was thirty years old and had raven-black hair. Her makeup, hair, and clothing were always impeccably done. She had a style that other woman always noticed and admired. I was older than Dee and often copied her fashion. I admired her level of energy. She not only devoted time to herself but managed to get her three

Dee, education and marketing coordinator

Joel, maintenance supervisor

Tom, reptile keeper

Chris H., reptile keeper

Historic Conestoga wagon placed in Wolf Woods in preparation for the coming wolves.

children ready for school all before arriving to work by 7:30 a.m., usually carrying a basket of warm goodies. Dee spoiled the staff, and we loved her for it.

Dee's mind drifted. *What would they look like?* she wondered. *Would they be friendly?* Her kids had been pestering her about how soon they could go to work with her and see the wolves. She knew once the wolves were there, attendance would swell. This would help secure everyone's jobs, which tended to be precarious at such a small, underfunded zoo.

Joel instructed his two helpers Tom and Chris to take hold of each end of the rickety, historic Conestoga wagon.

"When I give the word, you guys push and I'll pull. I want it wheeled next to the mound. It'll give the exhibit that *Little House on the Prairie* look. Okay … ready … let's heave-ho!" Joel boomed.

"I don't think it's gonna fit through the gates," Tom objected.

"I'll bet my Harley on it that it will, so just push harder," Joel replied. He always felt with enough force anything would fit, and if not, he would make it. Inevitably he proved himself right.

Heritage Zoo entrance. The Reptile Building is on the left.

Joel's strength amazed us. His average-sized physique was deceptive; on many occasions he pushed his body to lift weights well beyond what we all thought possible. In spite of his outer appearance—long flowing ponytail, leather vest, and biker boots—Joel had a spiritual side. The tiny gold cross pinned to his vest contrasted with his roaring motorcycle entrances, giving the impression that there was more to Joel than initially assumed. We considered him the zoo pastor because he always offered insight on how to deal with inner turmoil and was willing to drop whatever he was doing to help his co-workers. Wolf Woods was Joel's pet project. He had labored over it, when time and revenue allowed, for three years. More than anyone else, he beamed with pride as it neared completion.

"Now come on, let's do it," Joel urged. The three men grunted, groaned, pushed, and prodded until the wagon was through the gates.

"All right, we're in. Now, Dale wants it over there," Joel pointed toward the knoll. After more shoving and jostling, the wagon was finally in its designated spot.

The sky clouded over, and an early evening wind swirled around as Tom slipped a shiny brass lock on the outer exhibit door.

"Looks pretty good, don't you think, Joel?" he asked, although it was more a statement than a question.

"Yup. We've done an awesome job. They should do really well in here. I wonder how close they are," Joel said as he glanced over Tom's shoulder toward the park's entrance, not expecting to see the white van in the distance but hoping all the same.

"I'm going to close up the herpetarium. Radio me as soon as you see 'em," Tom said.

"Sure thing," Joel answered.

Tom, a young man with a thirst for reptile knowledge, had been instrumental in upgrading the herpetarium, which housed a variety of snakes and amphibians. It was many students' favorite building during field trips. However, most teachers and parents did not share their children's enthusiasm. Often parents, particularly mothers, insisted on standing outside while their children visited the creatures inside.

The fear of reptiles and also their persecution originally comes from simultaneous disgust and fascination, along with ignorance as well as age-old cultural stories and religious beliefs. The Old Testament story of Adam and Eve's expulsion from Eden implicates a snake in the greatest downfall of mankind. Once nicknamed "messengers of darkness," they were associated with mystical powers and sinister forces. The snake's hidden life, legless and silent movement, and forked tongue all arouse human suspicion. Conversely, however, this reviled creature is also a symbol for healing; the Aesculapian snake coiled around a staff is an emblem of medicine.

It is left to the individual to choose between negative or positive attitudes toward reptiles, and what to pass on to the next generation. Will the child learn to appreciate and value reptiles, or choose instead to smash a snake with a shovel, stuff a firecracker inside a frog's mouth, or drive over a basking turtle with an ATV? We, and our children, can choose a naturalist role, to be guardians of our planet's wildlife, respecting all living things from the tiniest toad to the wondrous wolf. Attitude will determine the fate of the earth's flora and fauna. 🐾

Columbian boa constrictors.

Chapter 2

The Heritage Pack

"Only a half hour and we'll be there, Dorth," Dale said, calling me by my nickname, which I had gotten when we were first dating and happened to be watching *The Wizard of Oz*. Precisely how it came to be is no longer clear in my mind, but it has stuck over the years, and it is the name I sign his cards with.

"How are they doing?" he asked.

"I'm sure they'll be glad to get out of those crates," I answered. "I know I'll be glad—the smell is really getting to me." We had spent two weary days driving from Montana to Nebraska, only stopping to water the wolves and take a few rest breaks. Plus, there was the added challenge of not getting too nauseated from the odor of carnivore feces in a closed van.

"I can't wait to see how they like their new home. I'm getting so *excited*," I chattered. I spun in my seat to face our Akita who was curled up on the floor behind me. "What do you think, Poocha Bear, are you getting excited too?" Her brown eyes glanced up at me, confused. She stood and head-butted my hand in hopes of receiving a loving pat. I could not resist and petted her velvety head.

It had been a peculiar trip for Bear as well. She had spent the past forty-eight hours sleeping next to her distant, wilder relatives, separated by welded steel bars and a thin wool blanket. The wolves and Bear could smell and hear one another. These two senses, essential to a wolf's survival, make them amazingly efficient hunters. Their olfactory sense has been estimated to be one hundred times more acute than that of humans. Wolf expert L. David Mech reported in *The Wolf: The Ecology and Behavior of an Endangered Species* that the scent of a cow moose with twin calves was picked up by wolves more than four miles away, and author R.D. Lawrence wrote in *Wolves* that a five-month-old wolf pup could smell a porcupine eating grass in a meadow a mile away.

After smell, hearing is a wolf's keenest sense. Mech reported that "wolves can hear as far as six miles away in the forest and ten miles away on the open tundra."

These two senses offset a wolf's mediocre eyesight. Visually, wolves see no better than humans, but in a two-seat van, they did not need raptor vision to spot a dog like Bear. We had tossed a blanket over the

The author with her husband Dale, director of Heritage Zoo.

crates to help minimize the animals' stress levels. We certainly did not want a clash of teeth breaking out as we drove along Interstate 90.

As the day wound down, only two staff remained at the zoo and they were getting restless.

"What time is it?" Joel asked.

"Ten past six," Tom answered.

"If they don't get here soon, it'll be dark and that'll make things real interesting," Joel mumbled while he paced. Just seconds after he spoke, a horn blew repeatedly off in the distance. They turned toward the noise.

"Here they come. I'll get the back gate," Joel yelled cheerfully, his feet already moving him toward the gate as his words drifted back to Tom. Tom did a quick double check of the emergency capture equipment strewn at his feet: tranquilizer gun, CO_2 canister, catch strap, leather gloves, fire hose, and ropes to hold the kennel doors ajar. He was satisfied that he had everything ready.

Joel flung the gate open, allowing the van to peel through. I smiled and waved, hoping he would forgive us for the dust cloud that kicked up in his face. Dale drove faster than necessary, apparently impatient to unload the precious cargo before daylight was gone. After pushing himself these last few days for the benefit of the animals, he was a man with a single-minded focus. If he wanted to catapult the van over the zoo's swan creek, I was all for it. Thankfully though, he chose to stick to the road. The pair of mute swans that routinely claimed the road as their dominion this time of day flapped in annoyance as we accelerated past them. The van came to a gravel-skidding halt just inches from Tom. If he had not jumped to the side, the Ford logo would have become his new belt insignia.

I unbuckled my seat and delighted in a much-needed stretch. Dale, on the other hand, did not even turn the ignition off before he got out.

"Boy, is he wired," I mumbled.

"Hi! Welcome home. How was the trip?" Tom asked cheerfully.

The author's dog, Bear.

"Long, very long," Dale answered. I reached over and turned off the van. As I fumbled under my seat for Bear's leash, she managed to squeeze her sixty-pound body between the two captain's seats and plop herself in my lap with her front paws pressed against the dash. She wanted a better glimpse of the person standing next to Dale.

"Bear … just wait a minute," I muttered, as I clamped her leash to her collar. I opened my door only to have her vault over my lap and onto the ground.

"Geez … Dale, grab her," I grumbled, as the leash slipped from my hand. She jumped up on Tom in record time. Bear was a very affectionate dog—far too sociable to be a guard dog. She befriended everyone enthusiastically. Fortunately, Tom had dogs of his own, so he did not mind.

"Okay, Bear, that's enough," I said as I picked up her leash. "Give Tom a break." Tom smiled and gave Bear one last scratch behind her ear.

"She'd have you do that 'til the sun goes down … which I guess is right about now," I said, laughing at my own joke. Joel sauntered up to Dale.

"Hey, Boss. That should hold 'em, don't ya think?" Joel boasted as he motioned to the twelve-foot exhibit fence.

"Well, we'll see," Dale casually responded. It certainly was not the vote of confidence Joel was hoping for, but that was Dale's way.

Captive wolves have been known to jump over exhibit walls, dig out, or chew through cage mesh. Dale never underestimated an animal's tenacious desire for freedom or ruled out the possibility that the animal might locate a weakness in the structure that had been overlooked by the builders. He had witnessed astonishing escapes many times in his zoo career. A spectacled caiman crocodilian was found lounging on top of its aquarium four days in a row (eventually named Houdini); a Lowland silverback gorilla was discovered in the keeper alley totally enthralled with ripping apart a phone book. An emu loped along a grassy back road with no intention of returning to its yard, and a blood python was found sprawled under the driver's seat next to the floor heater during a midnight transport. Dale was never convinced an exhibit was escape-proof until time proved it so.

"Let's unload all the crates first, then we'll decide what order to release them in," Dale commanded. Tom slid the side van doors open while Dale and Joel unlatched the trailer doors. Even though the excitement was mounting and I wanted nothing more than to stay right where I was, my bladder said otherwise. I took Bear and headed to the bathroom inside the Commissary. North of the wolf exhibit, the Commissary building housed the small educational animals, had a quarantine area for the sick and injured, and was the keepers' diet prep kitchen.

"Come on, Bear, I'll race ya," I said. She sprang ahead and headed straight for the thirty mallard ducks that slept at the edge of the pond. I watched the

Tina, Solo's sister.

feathered chaos unravel. Bear bowled through the startled ducks, and they took to the sky like leaves caught in a gust of wind. Thankfully Bear proved herself a poor bird dog and missed every single one. I scolded myself for not anticipating her plot before she charged ahead.

This put a quick end to our playtime, and she whined as I tied her to the fence alongside the building. After a few minutes I was back with the men. As I pulled the blanket off Solo and Tina's cages, I was met by two sets of amber eyes. I stood quietly. Never had I been this close to such mesmerizing wild animals. I thought how odd it was that they were so calm. I expected something altogether different—more defensive posturing, or staying to the back of their kennel, or even a subtle growl to tell me, a stranger, to stand back. How unlike wolves they seemed to be. They were not lunging at the crate door nor snarling with teeth bared. The hair on their hackles did not bristle. Their ears did not stick straight up in an aggressive position. They were nothing like what I had expected. I had previously observed and studied the wolf packs at Calgary Zoo and Moose Jaw Zoo. At times those wolves had been relaxed and other times excited by human presence, but that was because they were in their environment and comfort zone. These wolves were not in either zone. I was eager to start studying these fascinating and mysterious animals.

I stepped to the back of the trailer to check on the other two. Shilo looked cramped and agitated. Her two-day ordeal had been miserable, compounding her already weakened physical state. When we left the Triple D Ranch, she was gaunt and her fur patchy and dull. Her ivory-yellow eyes were not a deep golden tint like the others', which worried me. I would later learn that wolves' eyes take on a wide range of yellow hues and occasionally even remain blue after the wolf reaches maturity.

Shadow and Shilo's traveling trailer was cloaked in total darkness. In order for both crates to fit in the trailer, we had to slide Shilo's on its side, leaving no space above her head when she sat up. She soon realized that lying down was her only option if she wanted any form of comfort. When we lifted her crate from the vehicle, her lean 73-pound body was in dire need of sunlight, food, and exercise. With her head lowered and body crouched, she looked scared and vulnerable. I spoke quietly to her and tried to convey that everything would be fine and that soon she would be out and running with the others. Though I never expected it, her body language was evident of things to come—she would display this same fearful posturing throughout her life with the pack.

It took thirty minutes to unload all four crates and in that time we shared the incredible thrill of being within inches of wolves. There is no doubt that when you stare into the eyes of a wolf, you are instantly humbled. Dale is not one to reveal his emotions but even he teared up as he stood next to Solo.

The wolves had never been housed together, so Dale felt it did not matter what order they were released into the exhibit. As chance would have it, Solo would be the first, forecasting her future role in the pack. She bolted from the crate faster than my five-hundredth-of-a-second shutter speed could capture. Tina showed less panic to break from her two-day home. It took her several minutes to decide to explore her new surroundings. Shilo could not wait to escape her metal prison. Her crate door was barely half open when she darted through it, scraping her back along the steel stripping. We kept Shadow in his kennel while we discussed his release. He was only four months old, had been raised alongside

Shilo—thin, frail, and scared.

Solo, leaving her crate and entering the Wolf Woods exhibit.

a family dog, and had never been exposed to other wolves. We had two equally attractive options: introduce him to the adult females slowly over the next few weeks, or put him in with them that night to begin pack bonding. We decided on the latter.

The exhibit was new territory for all four animals, so no individual animal had prior claim to the area and there was no previous hierarchy. In theory, there should have been little or no aggression among them. We swung Shadow's door open. He showed no interest in leaving the security of his kennel but instead sat contently, staring out. Then he caught sight of Tina running laps around the juniper bush and the puppy within him surfaced. He shot out after her. He knew exactly how to introduce himself. He dropped on his side and exposed his groin and stomach, exhibiting totally submissive behavior. It was a very good sign.

Solo, Tina, and Shilo explore their new space.

The pack: Shadow, Solo, Tina, and Shilo.

I burned through a role of film as the wolves paraded past. Each wolf crisscrossed the others as they investigated what their noses picked up. I turned to Dale.

"They're absolutely beautiful, aren't they?" I sighed. Shilo ran up and over the lookout hill, then belly-crawled into the den. Tina squatted and marked the ground beneath the birch tree while Solo jumped into the back of the wagon and rolled in some fetid pile that only a wolf would find so irresistible. Suddenly, as though directed by instinct, they converged for an affectionate greeting. It was nature at its best. They licked one another's muzzles, rubbed bodies, and moved in unison around the base of the oak. The Heritage Pack was born. 🐾

Chapter 3

Finding Her Place

From the first day the wolves arrived, the keepers entered their exhibit in pairs, but that did not satisfy me. I felt the presence of another person would somehow take away from my experience with them.

At an earlier staff meeting the discussion of going into the wolf exhibit alone had been addressed, and since I was the wolves' primary caretaker and voiced the strongest desire to do so, entering their surroundings unaccompanied would fall to me.

I partially wanted to go in by myself for selfish reasons, for the sheer thrill. But another reason is that I wanted to see if I could feel a kinship with them, something that might be hard to develop if I weren't alone with them. From my very earliest years, getting to know farm animals and even once having an adorable kitten of my very own, I have felt tremendously attached to the animal world. I have immense respect and adoration for animals, and I like to think they can sense that about me.

Five days had passed since the wolves had claimed Wolf Woods as their new home, and I was eager to be a part of their world, to be alone with the pack. The evening air gave me a boost of confidence. It was 6:30 p.m. and Dale was off checking the lemur building, close enough that if something went wrong, my shouts would be heard. I walked along the front of the exhibit, sizing up the wolves. They were resting and enjoying the drop in temperature. They calmly watched me walk past. I got to the gate and put my key in the lock. Then I took it back out.

"Okay, Sandra, you can do this. Would Dian Fossey back down? Of course not," I said to myself as I thought about my idol, who had courageously studied gorillas in Rwanda. I put the key back in, turned it, and stepped inside. The wolves stayed where they were. What a relief. I could not have continued if they came at me too quickly. My heart raced. I took a deep breath and moved toward the oak tree. I hoped the wolves viewed my movements as confident, that was the vibe I was trying for, although my weak knees fought it. I got to the stump and sat down. All four wolves got up, which immediately triggered a nervous habit of mine, picking the skin on my thumbs until they bleed. I'm sure at that point, I looked far from confident. Within seconds, three of them surrounded me. Solo came up behind and nudged her nose into my hair. Tina sniffed my shoes and Shadow touched my hand. I was convinced the blood on my thumbs was the reason for his interest.

I fervently wished I had kicked the habit years earlier as I waited for him to react to fresh blood. I continued to hold my breath and stayed motionless. A second turned to minutes as they continued to check me out as they might another wolf. I slowly, *slowly* relaxed. My heart rate slowed and I unclenched my fists, which by now had made fingernail dents in my palms. I sat with the wolves for about half an hour, more than enough time for them to smell every inch of me and for me to meet the pack. Shilo never greeted me that night. I grabbed the bite stick lying at my feet and stood to leave. Solo, Tina, and Shadow escorted me back to the gate. Shilo remained behind and smelled the stump. I locked their cage and ran like a child to tell Dale.

Midmorning a week later, the media scrambled for prime viewing positions in front of Wolf Woods. Dale was on the walkway giving an interview to one of the local TV stations. For Grand Island, this was big news. Not even the prestigious Omaha Zoo had gray wolves at that time.

The wolves' presence created an infectious excitement. They are a species that stirs both fear and fascination within people, much the way snakes do. We seem innately drawn to things that are capable of killing us, but at the same time we are determined to eliminate those threats out of fear.

"Do wolves eat people?" "Do they kill just because they like to?" "Can they really hypnotize a person just by looking at them?" These were a few of the questions we were asked that morning. They were indicators of the neuroses, fascination, and lack of knowledge people still had of these elusive predators.

Zoos play a vital role in breaking down prejudices and addressing the fear of wolves in a rational and responsible manner. Using interpretive talks, public wolf howls, artifacts, and current educational material, we correct the many myths surrounding wolves to help shape a healthier view of predators. Most zoos achieve their goals, especially among open-minded young people, but some people seem determined to stick with an old belief. Reshaping views on wolves depends a great deal on geography. If a person's home and work is in an area where wolves range, then he is personally affected by these predators, unlike a city dweller whose infatuation is from afar. It is the classic not-in-my-backyard situation; the further one is from the issue, the easier it is to be on the side of wildlife.

I found this to be true three years later when I submitted an editorial to a local Montana paper in favor of wolves. I received nasty letters back from several Helena residents objecting to my opinion because I did not live in "wolf

At four months old, Shadow was the pack's pup.

country." I had to concede; they did have a legitimate argument. I began to be more objective toward those who oppose wolves in their neighborhood. Since then, whenever I gave speeches on wolves, I explained both sides of the story. I tried to state the facts and let my audience decide. I did, however, always end my presentations by emphasizing that over six billion humans have been moving into the animals' neighborhood, not the other way around, and that respect and tolerance for all creatures is imperative to coexisting on our shared planet.

Regardless of one's individual attitude toward them, wolves are an undeniably critical part of their natural habitat—in fact, they are a measure of a healthy such ecosystem. "If you see wolves there, that wilderness is intact," according to Canadian wolf biologist Paul Paquet.

The Heritage Pack wolves were notably agitated the morning of the news conference, pacing along the back fence line. The bustle of people, the noise level, and all the camera gear aimed at them like telescopic guns seemed to upset them. We were encroaching on their "flight distance"—the distance between an animal and the source of danger. Shadow chose to retreat to the den and not show his face. Shilo was the most nervous. She ran frantically back and forth in the far corner trying desperately to distance herself from the loud, scary commotion. People's direct gazes made her feel like she was being stalked and elicited an escape reaction. Unfortunately, there was no place for her to go. Tina and Solo were also distressed.

I tossed each of them a steak. I thought it might help them relax and make them more visible to the interviewers, but not even choice T-bones enticed them.

The wolves had spent most of their lives in single kennel runs, deprived of physical contact with other wolves before coming here. Since cameras had shaped their former lives, the wolves were rightfully cautious of the roaming camera crews. They had not been at their new home long, so their agitation was understandable. I felt bad though, as if I had betrayed them. I had just begun to gain their trust and to be accepted into their environment, and there I was, a pivotal part of what they felt was a stressful confrontation. I wanted to

Shilo, the pack's omega wolf.

somehow tell them that they were not in harm's way, that shortly the strangers would be gone, and that their day would return to normal.

By 10:30 a.m. the film crews had shot their footage, demolished two dozen donuts and a pot of coffee, and left to cover some other story. It was early afternoon before I was able to return to the wolves. I unlocked their exhibit and went inside. Shadow was quick to venture out of the den once he saw me walk by its opening. I sat on the log next to the oak tree and watched as Solo and Tina searched for the tasty meat pieces I had thrown earlier. Shilo remained curled in the far corner with her eyes alert, darting from side to side, ready to jump to her feet if need be. She had exerted a lot of energy that morning and needed to regain her strength.

It took very little coaxing to get Shadow to amble over. With his head bent down and tilted to the side, he was ready for me to stroke his fur. He enjoyed my massaging his neck and belly, and I enjoyed the privilege as well. I cherished each time one of the wolves allowed me that closeness.

When Tina saw me petting Shadow, she dropped her bone and came over. She straddled my legs and placed her front paws on the log so her face was level with mine. I made sure my eyes looked past, and not at, hers. Giving the cue of a challenge would be dangerous. I slid my arm between her front legs and rubbed her chest. My heart pounded, due to both the thrill of being so intimate with a wolf and also from an uneasiness—I remembered reading that wolves' jaws have five times greater biting power than a German shepherd's. I was just inches away from that kind of strength.

Tina, the pack's beta wolf.

As Tina's breath fanned my cheek, another thought entered my mind. Prior to the animals arriving at the zoo, my experience with wolves was from a safe distance—nothing as intimate as this. I marveled at my own daring, or maybe it was stupidity. I just knew those past weeks had profoundly altered my life and given me back a family I desperately needed. They made me feel happy again.

Thirteen months earlier I had stood at the bottom of the Saskatchewan airport escalator waiting for my daughter to return to me from her summer with her father. One passenger after another walked past me. Even the flight attendants, who normally ushered her to me, walked past with no young girl holding their hands. Amanda never appeared. Panic shifted to sorrow, which shifted to betrayal when hours later I learned she would not be coming back to me. Amanda would stay with her father. August 1994 saw a light in my heart go out. In September 1995, the wolves turned it back on.

Throughout the '70s and '80s my connection with animals was confined to weekends and vacations—photographing waterfowl, grizzly bears, herds of elk, bighorn sheep, etc. Not until I moved out west in the mid-1980s, much to the chagrin of several family members, was I able to nurse my addiction for wildlife.

Early on, Amanda learned the wonders of nature. As a single parent, I spent weekends hiking and bird watching with her. She was proud of her bright yellow Fisher-Price binoculars. We woke up at 3 a.m. many Saturday mornings and drove north to the provincial park to arrive at its gates by dawn. When she was five I gave her a camera so she could take wildlife pictures. She loved to be creative and most times tilted her camera forty degrees to achieve abstract images.

But it was when I finally got a job at the Calgary Zoo in Alberta, Canada, that we were both truly thrilled. She bragged to her friends about where her mom worked and she got to go behind-the-scenes to touch the animals. The job allowed me to see, hear, and smell creatures from around the globe, although it still wasn't ideal since I held an office job. At least it got me near animals. But not even nine hours a day were enough; as often as I could, I hiked on the trails in Fish Creek Park and the Kananaskis Mountain range. During summers, when Amanda stayed with her father in Ontario, I traveled to far-off places to photograph polar bears on the barren tundra, harp seals on the pack ice, or wildebeest on the Serengeti.

Solo, the pack's alpha wolf.

Vacations, I realized, were not going to cut it in the long run. So even though I had gone to college for business, I knew I had to start preparing for my real calling: zookeeper. I attended seminars by wolf biologist Paul Paquet, read all the latest wolf journals from field researchers, enrolled in OPC (operant conditioning) workshops, and took numerous courses to qualify as an Animal Behaviorist. All of this prepared me for the day I stepped through the gates of Wolf Woods.

When working with animals, accurately interpreting their behavior is necessary to remain safe. One should be sincerely sensitive to an animal's needs and perspectives. As our time together continued, I believed the wolves regarded me as a member of their pack, although they never rivaled me in a rank order match. This concept, viewing human behavior in terms of animal behavior, is known as zoomorphism; the human's attitude does not impede the success of interacting with animals. It teaches people to ask, what does the animal make of the situation? Anthropomorphism is the opposite—people assume animals operate similarly to humans and then make assumptions based on what humans need, not what the animal needs.

When I entered their world, since they were still adapting to their new habitat and establishing a hierarchy, I could move about unharmed. I could not wait to enter the wolf classroom every day and learn more about them. I was turning into a fanatic.

Even though the wolves enjoyed interacting with me, they obviously reveled in frolicking with each other. Shadow would latch onto Tina's tail and tug, while she gently took hold of his neck fur. Each took a turn at mouthing the other's legs, tail, and neck. It seemed their only mission was to explore and revel in the fun of pack life.

Often I tried to photograph them but was unsuccessful since my camera strap proved too tempting a chew toy and the camera lens inevitably ended up with nose prints. As soon as I would place my equipment outside their exhibit, they practically posed for great photographs. It was as though they understood the irony of it. Another lesson I learned was a painful one—always tuck your ponytail inside your shirt. Wolves view any loose piece of clothing, any shiny, dangling object (keys, earrings, boot laces) as the makings of a tug-o'-war, and they always win. My shredded shirts, bent keys, and fewer strands of hair can attest to that.

Shadow, the black pup of the group, was always eager to spend time with me, and I rewarded him with a head scratch. And even though he was the youngest, he held his own during feedings. Frequently, he kept both Tina and Shilo back while he ate his fill.

Solo's sister Tina was an attractive grizzled color, with distinctive saddle markings running along her back. She and Solo were fortunate to grow up together in the Kalispell kennel, which allowed them to develop as healthier wolves. They had not been kept isolated like Shilo. Even though she and Solo were the same age, Tina settled into the beta position, the second ranking wolf. She lost fights to Solo, the alpha, but won over the others. Tina tended to get more to eat than Shilo but not as much as Solo and Shadow. Shadow was allowed to eat first alongside Solo because he was the pup and a pack nurtures its young.

Tina let me enter her space and was the first of the wolves to lick my mouth, which is a friendly way of saying hello. People may be grossed out by the thought of a wolf kiss, but to me it was an exclusive honor. Nothing is quite as exhilarating. Tina was selective about who she liked and nipped at anyone who entered her enclosure, except me.

Tina.

Solo stands on what was eventually called "Solo's Summit."

Solo was by far the most striking of all four wolves. In her thick, cream-colored fur coat, she patrolled her domain like a queen. She was confident and stayed in peak condition by dominating feeding sessions, allowing only Shadow close to her and the food. Winning all the fights, Solo clearly held the alpha position, although Shilo seemed driven to challenge her every chance she got. When I entered Solo's realm, she remained aloof and did not allow me to touch her. It was as though I had not yet proved myself worthy.

Shilo, who had arrived emaciated, had begun to gain some weight, but her fur remained sparse. She was the oldest of the wolves, and studies show that as wolves age, their fur lightens. Shilo's whitish-tan coat certainly supported that.

Oddly enough, gray wolves are not necessarily gray but rather, a combination of color hues varying from eggshell white to rusty brown to charcoal.

Shilo's prior life of neglect and little social contact with other wolves, created a restless, mistrusting, fearful animal. She was, by all definitions, the underdog. Probably that is what endeared me to her from the start. She needed to belong, to be a part of a pack, to have a wolf's life, and I wanted to help her.

Socializing wolves to humans has been thoroughly recorded by Dr. Erich Klinghammer, Director of Wolf Park in Battle Ground, Indiana. He has written of the importance of socializing captive wolves. This ensures the animals are not fearful of humans, so routine medical and other handling procedures can be done with little trauma to the wolf and thus less disruption to the pack's social order. Socialization also encourages animals to behave normally, interact with each other, and remain relaxed during human activity in and around their enclosure.

The socializing process begins at a very young age. The pup is separated from the mother after ten to fourteen days and then lives twenty-four hours a day with human foster parents. Klinghammer's approach has proved quite successful with gray wolves. Similar techniques are used with other animals, usually animals that are rejected by their mothers or orphaned. It is referred to as imprinting. Unfortunately, however, once imprinted, there is little chance the animal can be released back into the wild. It is destined for a life in captivity.

Socializing wolves renders two main benefits: safety and enrichment for the animal. Socializing allows the keeper full contact with the animal without the danger of injury. Also, when the animal is socialized, time spent with human companions is a rewarding time for the wolf. The animal is exposed to stimuli such as human touch, an occasional walk outside of the wolf's normal environment, and new and different pack members to interact with. These activities provide for the psychological well-being of the animal and phase out stereotypical behavior such as: excessive pacing, self-mutilation, over-grooming resulting in hot spots, repeated yawning, and frequent food caching.

There was evidence the Heritage Pack had been socialized to some degree in the past but not to the full recommended extent. Some pack members were more approachable than others. The most anxious wolf Shilo had not been pulled from her mother until she was as old as twenty-one days or more. Studies show that once the pups' eyes are open, they are fearful of humans. Trying to get the wolf to overcome this fear is time-consuming and socialization often fails.

It was mid-October, and Dale and I had just arrived back from a week in Canada. I was worried the wolves may have forgotten who I was. I could not wait to see them. I made Dale unpack the car while I grabbed my camera and went over to the zoo just after 5 p.m. They appeared placid and settled in their new home. As they chewed on bits of meat from an earlier feeding, their eyes followed me as I walked toward the stump under the oak. When the staff interacted with the pack, we sat in the same designated spot to ensure the wolves understood the purpose for entering their enclosure. Within minutes Shadow and Tina trotted over. Solo began circling me but far enough away that I was still unable to touch her. Shilo did the same, although tonight she was different. She made eye contact with me and inched closer but still kept a cautious distance.

I felt giddy, like I had just received the best Christmas present ever, when the wolves came over to greet me. It would be silly to say I had forgotten what beautiful animals they were since I was only gone a week, but somehow I felt like I was seeing them for the first time. I watched their faces change expression as they interacted. I studied the variation of color in their gorgeous coats and paid close attention to the determination of their movements. Everything about them fascinated me.

They only stayed for a short time and then returned to their scraps of meat. About ten minutes later, Shilo came back carrying a large bone and laid it two feet in front of me. I took several photos of her until the sound of the shutter eventually disturbed her. It was a rare moment; Shilo seemed content and relaxed to chew her bone so close to me. Eventually she tired of her bone and gave it up to Tina but continued to stay with me. And if Tina had not body-pressed her (the animal comes in on the side and leans into the shoulder area of the other, keeping its head, ears, and tail high) she may have stayed longer but instead she moved away. It was a definite beginning for Shilo and me. I left their exhibit and walked home happily flushed with endorphins. They had not forgotten me.

Just as Tina accepted her position in the pack, Shilo refused to resign herself to the lowest ranking role: the omega. Almost from the beginning, Solo made sure Shilo was denied any form of normal family life. Solo growled and bared her teeth at Shilo. As the omega, Shilo was forced to eat last, if allowed to eat at all, and prevented from rallying with the pack for body rubs. Shilo often watched from a distance as the others merged and howled together. Shilo's howl was a haunting, solitary call. She cried out to be accepted.

Even Solo's physical attacks did not deter Shilo from rivaling for a higher place within the family. She had not endured all those years of hardship just to

Shilo in a rare moment of contentment.

end up at the bottom. She seemed driven to fight Solo for the top. But finding her place, or accepting her place, would not come without a price.

Late one afternoon a week after returning from Canada, I had an exceptional surprise. I sat under the tree and called to Shadow. He immediately walked over, rather slowly, head swinging and looking like a clumsy puppy. He was never too busy eating or too comfortable to spend time with me. He stood at my feet while I rubbed his head and back and then buried my face in his shoulder fur. It was incredible that I felt safe enough to put my face so close to a wolf's face. Tina and Solo joined us. I was rubbing Tina's side when suddenly, for the first time, Solo stood next to me so I could stroke the top of her head. I kept my own head low and eyes on the ground. The other two walked off but Solo stayed. I felt so honored, as though she finally granted me passage into her wolf world. Only a few other times in my life have I felt such a deep, humbling emotion: once when

Solo.

I met civil rights leader Nelson Mandela, again with archaeologist Mary Leakey, and lastly with primatologist Dr. Jane Goodall.

As intense as my interaction with Solo was, I greedily craved more. I also wished Shilo could be a pack participant instead of just an observer.

The very next day there was obvious tension between the wolves. I fed them their morning meal but only three of them ate. Shilo stayed back. I tossed her a piece that landed directly at her feet. She snatched it and ran to the far corner where she kept looking up the entire time she ate. It was not until I cleaned their pool that I noticed she was bleeding. As I got closer I saw several cuts on her left hind leg, and right front leg. Within seconds of my noticing her injuries, she began pacing and then ran crazed along the fence with her tail tight between her legs. The other three were now crowding in on her as though they were trying to chase her out. I quickly moved back toward the pool hoping the three would follow behind me. They did. This gave Shilo some temporary relief. The reason for her frenzied behavior was clear. They had attacked her just hours earlier, and she anticipated another attack.

By midday I witnessed another intense clash that left Solo with a deep bite on her left eye. It bled extensively and later swelled shut. Surprisingly, Shilo fared quite well, although she whimpered and displayed submissive tail-tucking much of the afternoon. However, by early evening she acted more assertive, coming up to the gate with the others for food. She actually ate the most, and as I was leaving she stood confidently on Solo's Summit, which Solo tolerated. Evidently Shilo had been victorious, but one success did not guarantee her the role of leader.

In spite of Shilo's small victory the day before, it became obvious something had to be done. The dynamics between Solo and Shilo heightened into daily clashes. It is unusual for pack members to fight when it is not linked to feeding or breeding. Their conflicts erupted after little provocation. We decided to move Shilo into a separate area for a short time. Even though it was for her own protection, we felt as though we were breaking her spirit. We were stripping her of pack life and throwing her back into the isolation she had languished in for years before joining the Heritage Pack. Were we doing the right thing? If we were, why did it feel so wrong? 🐾

Chapter 4

The Family Shadow

There was no indication Shadow was feeling sick that November morning. As with all wild animals, showing signs of weakness or illness does not serve them well. Survival depends on their ability to disguise poor health. Shadow stood by the gate with the others as they waited for their morning meal. He did appear less enthusiastic, but I paid little attention. I assumed he was just not overly hungry.

I certainly made sure the wolves were well fed. They each got two to three pounds of commercially packaged raw meat, usually beef or horse, and periodically during the fall, hunters would donate portions of their deer carcasses. On those occasions I would explain to the zoo visitors the complex social interactions at the "kill," like who tears into the carcass first. Who gets to eat and who might go hungry.

Wild wolves sometimes lose their kill to other hungry predators; so when they do get to eat, they eat a lot. That is why wolves stomachs are large and adapted to storing anywhere from six to thirty-five pounds of food at one time, to be digested later. Carnivores like cougars and grizzlies differ somewhat. Although they also feed liberally on their kills, when full they cover it with dirt, leaves, and debris, and after several days return to their cache and continue to feed until the carcass is consumed down to its skeletal remains. Captive wolves do not need to gorge themselves because the risk of going hungry has been eliminated. Starvation is a very real threat for wild packs since their success rate for taking down prey is 10 percent. Out of ten attempts, the wolves come away with only one meal, so when they are successful they rip into the flesh and feed voraciously.

I tossed the wolves their meat and proceeded to clean the exhibit. Shadow took his, headed over to the pine tree, and lay down. He kept it between his paws, apparently uninterested in eating but also unwilling to relinquish it. I thought nothing of it. The sun was warm that day and the whole pack lazed about. I finished cleaning and left the exhibit.

Erika walked in the back door of the office and stood next to the desk where I was writing my keeper notes. These

Shadow, chewing on a bone, November 1995.

Erika, raptor keeper

were a daily summary of health and behavioral observations of the animals in each keeper's section. I glanced up, and we stared silently at each other for an uncomfortable length of time. I wondered why she was not speaking.

"Hawk got your tongue?" I joked, since she was the raptor keeper. No response. "Okay, it wasn't one of my best jokes, but I think it at least deserves a smirk."

She hesitated awkwardly, then blurted out, "Shadow's dead."

My heart sank into my stomach.

"What are you saying?" I snapped. "I just saw him a little bit ago, and he was fine. That's a pretty sick prank, Erika, and I don't appreciate it."

"It's no joke. I really think he's dead," she repeated solemnly. Her eyebrows furrowed and her shoulders sank down.

"But how?" I asked, not wanting her to answer. I felt overwhelmed. Dazed, I tried to make sense of what she had just said, convinced she was wrong. Begging her to say no, I asked again. "Are you sure?"

"Yes. I'm so sorry. But I don't know what happened. I didn't go in. He's just lying next to the building," she said.

"Maybe he's just sleeping. He could be just sleeping," I whispered when she fell silent. She took my hand and squeezed it.

I radioed Dale to meet us at the wolf exhibit. We hurried down the pathway to Wolf Woods. It was strangely serene. How could an animal be dead and there be no sign of a struggle? I spotted him and immediately calmed down—I was certain he was napping. He was sprawled out, his back pressed against the fence, his head resting gently on its side. On cool days I often saw the wolves lying just that way, trying to expose their bodies to the maximum amount of sunlight. I called to him, but he remained still. That was not like him. Seldom, if ever, did I have to call twice to get his attention. I called out louder a second time. I refused to believe he was anything but sleeping.

"Come on, Shadow, nap time's over. Wake up, you lazy thing. I'll give you an extra belly rub if you get up." By then my talking had rallied all the wolves to the fence, except the one I wanted. I unlocked their cage and walked toward him, completely convinced he would raise his head and end this mean prank. I stood over him, the sun shining down on his ebony fur. As I knelt down and touched his velvety face, he remained motionless.

"Hi, my sweet boy. Come on, get up. Please don't leave me, Shadow." But after several agonizing moments, I knew it was true. Shadow was dead. But how? There were no signs of physical injury, no bite marks, nothing. If he had not been attacked by the others, then by what or whom? I feared that he had been poisoned or shot by some radical zoo visitor. I had heard of such things happening at other zoos. And yet there was no evidence of either. An hour earlier he had been fine, and now he was dead. It just made no sense. How could this be? Even Dale, who always seemed to have an answer for everything, could not understand this.

I had to get out of there. I could not stay and watch Dale and Erika remove his body from the exhibit. Helping to take him his family and home would have meant admitting he was gone.

I walked home, grief consuming me. His image flooded my mind and I could think only of his playful greetings and lumbering gait. Even though he had been with the pack a few short months, the pup had found a family. The pack's howls would be mournful that night.

Our veterinarian's necropsy later concluded that the "quiet killer" had struck. Canine parvovirus affects wolves, foxes, dogs, and other canines. There are two forms of CPV: gastrointestinal and cardiac, the intestinal being the most common. The intestinal lining is destroyed, leading to anemia and loss of protein; white blood cell levels drop, further weakening an already weak animal who is suffering from vomiting, dehydration, and diarrhea. The animal dies soon after the onset of the disease, as early as two days later.

The second, less common, form of CPV is cardiac, affecting puppies in utero or shortly after birth. That is the period when maternal antibody protection decreases and vaccinations have not yet adequately protected the pup against infection. The virus attacks the heart muscle and the canine dies suddenly of heart failure. Fortunately, due to widespread vaccination of breeding dogs, this form is rarely seen now.

The parvovirus disease was discovered in 1978 and has been a major threat to wild canine populations, and currently is the most common infectious disorder of dogs throughout the United States. It is transmitted by direct oral contact with infected feces, soil, or inanimate objects—such as cage floors, clothing, and food pans—carrying the virus. Pups six to twenty weeks old are most susceptible. We surmised Shadow had been exposed to it during his time in Kalispell, because (as we later learned) their adult dog had exhibited symptoms but recovered after receiving treatment.

Time seemed to be our enemy that fall. It ran out for Shadow, and the mounting tension between the remaining pack members gave me little time to dwell on his passing. I needed to redirect my attention to immediate issues with them. The weather was getting colder, which instigated frequent scent-marking and threatening outbursts among the wolves. The breeding season was near.

Solo (left), Tina (right), and Shilo (below), January 1996.

As I spent time with the pack, I learned their daily routines and how they interacted with each other. Their aggression levels differed depending on which pack member was involved in the conflict, what time of year it was and what position that member held in the pack.

That fall was my introduction to a pack's behavior as breeding season approached. The clashes I had witnessed between Solo and Shilo were trivial in comparison to what was to come. Tina took no part in the body-pressing, bared teeth, and growls. She seemed almost oblivious to the actions between the other two females. Perhaps Solo and Shilo's outbursts had not yet been serious enough for Tina to feel the need to defend her position as beta.

After Shadow's death Solo's softer side emerged. She seemed less oppressive, less focused on keeping Shilo in her place. She walked the exhibit with less bold authority. Sometimes she even allowed Shilo to venture past without a confrontation. Solo seemed to be mourning the loss of the male pack member.

As Thanksgiving approached, Solo reverted back to her tyrannical self, reaffirming her status as alpha. That fact was beat into Shilo just after the long weekend. The pack had no time to lick its collective chops after a feeding before Shilo dared to glance in Solo's direction. That was all it took and Shilo found herself slammed to the ground, Solo's feet planted firmly on her chest. Shilo immediately leaned her head back and exposed her throat to her leader. That was apparently still not enough, so she whined until Solo released her.

Over the next weeks Shilo repeatedly extended friendly overtures toward the dominant sisters. This active submission confirmed her role as omega. Solo's frequent "riding up" posture, in which she placed her forelegs across Shilo's shoulders, was an extra reminder of who fed first.

With each passing day, I felt closer to the three wolves, although sometimes I was not particularly fond of their actions. Often I felt Solo acted like a schoolyard bully, and I wanted to rush in and protect Shilo. Tina, if and when she got involved with pack dynamics, tended to follow her sister's lead. For the most part, though, Tina did not assert her dominance over Shilo, making her more likable.

The three remaining members of the pack.

Christmas came and went with little incident among the wolves. The three females had found a peaceful middle ground. Wolf Woods was pleasantly subdued.

One January morning, Dale was busy compiling his director's year-end reports when a sheriff in Montana called. The sheriff told Dale that he had a wolf kenneled in his jail. She had escaped from her owner, a private citizen, who had made the rash decision of getting the wolf because of the allure of owning something different. The wolf, named Cheyenne, had chewed through the hemp rope that shackled her to a tree. Freedom was hers, if for only a few days. No matter how hard we humans try the wild essence of a wolf cannot be conquered. A Russian proverb states, "You may feed the wolf as much as you like. He will always glance toward the forest."

The authorities found Cheyenne roaming the streets of Whitefish, Montana, a small town south of Big Mountain Ski Resort. They refused to return her to the irresponsible owner, so they called various facilities that might be interested in accepting her. If the sheriff could not find a willing recipient, Cheyenne would have to be euthanized.

After gathering more information, we found out that the wolf was Shadow's littermate. Dale mulled over the offer to take her. He hesitated because adding another female possibly meant more conflicts.

He called a staff meeting to discuss taking this animal. For me, the answer was a resounding yes. After all, she was Shadow's sister; it would feel as though Shadow was still with us. Others at the meeting were not so quick to answer for or against. Their skepticism helped me acknowledge that my emotions were incidental and that we needed to address the relevant issues like whether or not the pack would accept her.

After weighing the pros and cons, we decided to add Cheyenne to our wolf family. Her young age was the critical factor. Since she was a juvenile, and represented the future of the pack, they should prize and pamper her. A mature female would probably not have been welcomed into the pack. Studies at the Burger's Zoo in Arnhem, the Netherlands, determined that captive females, especially alpha females, tend to be very intolerant of other adult females, not only during courtship but also in situations such as feeding and howling.

Two weeks passed before she was flown to us. Dale and I stood outside the Omaha freight hanger in the frigid January air waiting for the cargo doors to open. My heart was pounding with anticipation.

"I wish they'd hurry up. I'm freezing out here," I grumbled to Dale as I hopped around and rubbed my hands together.

"The agent inside said they were just finishing up the paperwork. She should be moved to the platform any minute," Dale answered.

The overhead sliding door creaked as it slid along its iced track, and a shaft of light spilled onto the snow in front of me. Impatient for the door to open, I bent down to peer inside the room hoping to get a glimpse of her.

"There's the kennel. I can just about see her," I yelled to Dale.

The fellow handed Dale the transport papers to sign, then turned to me and said, "Are you folks from Canada?"

In the past I would have been surprised by a stranger's perceptiveness, but in the past nine months, numerous people had made that same conclusion based on the way I pronounce certain words. "Let me guess. It was the word 'about' that gave it away, right?" I said, pronouncing it *aboot*.

"You got it," the man replied.

"Geez, I really need to work on that." I repeated the word out loud so I could hear how quirky it sounded coming from my mouth. It still seemed fine to me, just like every other time I tried the very same test. I shrugged my shoulders and turned to Dale, "At least I don't say 'eh' after every sentence." Dale smiled but then quickly got back to business.

"Can we move this along?" Dale said huffily, trying to keep me and the guy on track.

"Sure thing," the man answered. "By the way, what kinda dog is that?" He was unaware of what cargo was inside the kennel because we kept that information a secret.

"A very novel dog," Dale responded casually.

"Seems friendly enough," he added. "Not that I'd put my hand in there and test that, mind ya." He chuckled to himself.

"Well, we've got a long drive ahead of us, so let's get her loaded," Dale said.

The man was trying to be sociable, maybe to show us foreigners how friendly Americans could be. Or maybe the conversation was rescuing him from a long and lonely shift.

Either way, at least talking with him got my mind off the cold. We eased the kennel into the back of the van and waved goodbye to the fellow as he walked back inside the cargo bay.

"Look at those eyes—they're hypnotic," I said to Dale. She was black with dappled streaks of silver running through her fur.

"Hi, Cheyenne, you gorgeous thing. Let's get you home," I softly said.

The staff was excited about Cheyenne's arrival. She helped us feel connected to Shadow. In the following weeks, she had plenty of company during the day; the zookeepers devoted their lunch breaks to sitting in with her and helping her acclimate to the new surroundings. But it was the Heritage Pack's approval of Cheyenne that was most critical. She was kept in the adjacent exhibit, which let

Cheyenne, the newest member of the pack.

the pack get to know her through the mesh barrier and safeguarded the wolves from harm.

February is not the ideal month to add a new wolf to an existing pack, since it is the height of the breeding season. Nevertheless, Cheyenne and the pack acted accepting and playful with each other, so we were confident the full contact introduction would go well.

Tom and I decided to accompany Cheyenne into the exhibit. Because scent is such an important aspect of pack-member recognition, Tina and Solo immediately sniffed Cheyenne. Overcome with excitement, Cheyenne lurched forward, appearing to invite the others to a game of tag. Shilo stayed off to the side and watched the trio race around the oak.

Once Solo left the threesome to lie down, Shilo felt safe to approach Cheyenne. By this time Cheyenne was scarcely aware of Shilo's presence because she was focused on digging up a dead mallard. The bird had made the fatal mistake of flying too low over the wolf exhibit early that morning as it was descending toward the lagoon. Cautiously Shilo came up behind Cheyenne and smelled her; Cheyenne remained still and allowed Shilo all the necessary time to approve of her as the new family member.

Evidently Cheyenne would replace Shadow as the neutralizer. Her adolescence and playfulness provided key elements that would harmonize the family. She was eager to join the pack and explore her role as part of the team, since her previous life as someone's pet had deprived her of pack life.

Winter, although a burden to many of the zoo animals, was no bother to the wolves. They are supremely adapted for cold weather with layers of fur including outer guard hairs that protect from snow and rain and soft under-fur that warms against the subzero temperatures. The pack spent much of February and March curled up in a snow bank with their faces buried in their thick ruffs and concealed from the slicing wind.

During cold months wolves display luxurious coats, but once warm weather approaches they start looking more like inner city strays. The transition between winter and summer coats is a long, drawn-out process; for weeks, they walk around with large wads of fur dangling like Spanish moss on a cypress limb.

Nature changes clothes as each season melds into the next; the transformation at the zoo was apparent even to casual observers. The zoo's lagoon began with few dozen resident ducks and quickly became crammed with migratory mallards hungry for some free cracked corn. The new clover brought out the secretive Eastern cottontail rabbits. First they would nibble on the sweet treat, then scamper off in search of a mate. But the true gauge of spring's presence was in the loud call of the conspicuous red-winged blackbird. Teetering on blades of switch grass, it proudly peeped, "Konk-la-ree." Its distinct song lifted the staff's winter blues and hinted that summer was close. 🐾

Solo greets Cheyenne.

Chapter 5

Puppy Love

Ever since Shadow's death, something was missing. Since the gender ratio was off balance, we believed males were needed to unify and strengthen the pack. This decision came long before Cheyenne was offered to the zoo, but we still felt strongly about it even after she arrived. With an all-female pack, a certain amount of conflict was likely, even in our large one-acre exhibit with several sheltered retreats.

Wolf Woods lacked a primary ingredient for a more stable pack life. Unlike herds of deer, elk, caribou, and bighorn sheep, whose males and females live apart most of the year, wolf packs comprise both sexes year round.

There are numerous variables that sway the ratio of a wolf pack from year to year. Litter size and sex of the pups of that year, member mortality and deposed pack members all influence the ratio.

Once we decided to obtain a pair of male wolves, the wait was not long. In the month before the pups' arrival, a letter from my mother, including a newspaper clipping, came in the mail. She had never understood why I wanted to work with dangerous animals. She would have much preferred that I follow her example and become a secretary. I did that for ten years but always yearned for a much different life. During the 1970s, zookeepers tended to be men, so it never occurred to me to venture into that field, plus back then I was insecure and lacked the courage to move to a different city. It took years but I finally found the gumption.

The article, sensationally titled "Woman Killed by Wolves," was about a 24-year-old wolf keeper who had been attacked by her captive pack. The incident was thoroughly investigated by Dr. Klinghammer, an authority on captive wolves and their behavior. The young woman had entered the wolf exhibit alone, presumably to familiarize herself with them. However, that in itself was extremely risky since neither she nor the animals were adequately habituated to one another—it was only being her fourth day on the job and only her second time in the wolf enclosure. This was an established, non-socialized pack and she was entering their territory. In the past the animals had always kept their distance when humans entered their fifteen-acre enclosure. That afternoon would be different.

It was presumed that she had stumbled over one of the numerous fallen trees and branches in the enclosure and fell, which triggered the wolves' instinct to attack. Several, if not all, of the wolves attacked and killed her. Her lifelong dream of working with wolves came to a sudden and horrific end. To add to this already tragic story, the next day all five wolves were destroyed.

At the time of this tragedy, April 1996, the only known human injuries or fatalities inflicted by wolves were by captive animals. There were no documented cases in which wild wolves ever attacked a human, which leaves one to wonder whether captive wolves are more dangerous. What kind of animal has emerged from our quest to develop a closer relationship with wolves?

Two years later, however, would tell a different tale of wild wolf-human attacks. During the afternoon of September 1998 in Algonquin Park, Ontario, a 1½-year-old boy sat playing at a campsite, his parents only twenty feet away. From out of the bushes emerged a wolf, and within seconds it had the child in its mouth. He held the boy for a moment, then tossed him to the ground but continued to circle the picnic table. The family eventually scared him off.

In April 2000 two young boys were play-acting on the outskirts of a logging camp in Yakutat in southeastern Alaska. When they saw the wolf, they ran but 6-year-old John Stenglein was knocked down and bitten on the back, legs, and buttocks. A neighbor's dog tried to rescue the boy but was driven back. The wolf returned to John; his cries brought adults running and they drove the wolf away.

On the night of July 2000 a wolf entered the campsite of 23-year-old kayaker Scott Langevin, on the shores of Vargas Island, British Columbia. He awoke at 2 a.m. to a dark wolf tugging on his sleeping bag. His yells spooked the wolf and the wolf stepped back, but not for long. A moment later the animal lunged at Scott, biting his head. His friends awoke and drove the animal off.

In November 2005 a geology student, Kenton Carnegie, was attacked and killed by wolves while hiking in remote Northern Saskatchewan. His death marked the first known North American incident of a healthy, wild wolf killing a human. But the story should not end there, nor does it. Further investigation into the attack confirmed the wolves had been fed intentionally and unintentionally by the locals. The wolves had lost their fear of humans and began to view them as a source of food. Habituation to humans became the springboard to tragedy. In all the above cases the offending wolves were destroyed and necropsies indicated all to be healthy animals. It was and still is perplexing to wolf biologists.

June 1st was approaching quickly, so I put my mother's concerned letter out of my mind and concentrated on getting everything ready for the wolf pups. They would stay in our house, which was directly across the street from the zoo. That was one of the added benefits of Dale's position as Director. We got to live in the zoo house, so every morning we woke to either the crooning of wolves or the distinctive call of the male peacocks. We felt like we were camping.

In the upcoming months, the pups' home would be our screened-in porch, making it convenient to frequently check on them throughout the day. Unfortunately, our cats would have to find an alternate refuge to carry out their squirrel-spying missions. Dale and I got to the Grand Island Airport early enough that we were able to park directly in front of the terminal, so we would not have to carry their kennel too far. The pups' flight was due in from Omaha in thirty minutes, plenty of time for us to grab something to eat. Since I have a serious addiction to Starbucks coffee and pastries, I headed straight for that stand. Dale does not share the same affliction; he is more of an iced-tea-and-omelet guy. Once that first sip of bold-blend elixir made its way down my throat, I felt revitalized and ready for the day.

Waiting patiently, or otherwise, is not strong virtue of mine, so the coffee helped focus my attention on something other than my watch. My cup was still half full when the plane arrived. In no time at all, we saw a kennel loaded onto the baggage trolley and driven over to the terminal.

"That's got to be them, let's go," I said excitedly, fueled by caffeine but also eager to see the new babies.

"It'll take them a few minutes, so just slow down," he smiled, realizing I was nowhere near able to slow down. Thankfully the airport was small so we did not have to go far to get to where they unloaded the pups. We expected the pups to be huddled at the back of their crate out of nervousness, but instead their little black faces were pressed up against the door trying to see everything and everyone.

No one can resist a cuddly puppy, and the attraction of a cute wolf pup is even stronger. Once people caught sight of the pair a crowd formed around their kennel. We did not want to be rude, but we did not want to overexcite the pups either, so we quickly picked up the kennel and left the terminal, much to the disappointment of many children. Once inside the van, though, it was my turn to ogle them.

"Yup, they're cute all right," I said to Dale. Obvious, I know.

"I don't know. I think they look a bit homely. Black and fluffy with big blue eyes. How ugly is that?" Dale said casually. I swatted his arm after realizing he was messing with me. We both laughed.

The pups were from separate litters but both were black. The black color phase wolf comprises about 30 percent of northern region wolf populations.

Five-week-old wolf pups are relatively large, compared with other canines, yet one pup was particularly small next to the other even though they were merely three days apart in age.

Because wolves only breed once a year—unlike domestic dogs that can breed year-round—all wolves are born in early spring. This birth coincides with ungulate (deer, moose, elk, caribou) birth cycles, providing wolf parents easier prey. It is primarily the alpha male and older pack members that do the hunting during the early weeks of pup births. Once the prey is killed, part of the carcass is brought back to the nursing female in the den.

I named the smaller wolf with the white patch on his chest Montana and the larger one with a slightly lighter black coat Chinook, after the warming breezes that navigate the Alberta Rockies.

Because of their young age, captive hand-reared wolves form an emotional attachment to their human caretakers. Their willingness to substitute human companions for fellow wolves is what led to the first canine domestication; that and someone, somewhere 50,000 years ago began to feed wolves resulting in a captive wolf population.

Within a few days, I noticed a few personality traits of each pup. Chinook was far more people-oriented. He demanded attention from me, while Montana was more reserved and independent. I predicted Montana would someday be the alpha male in the Heritage Pack. But that was a long way off.

That first night was a sleepless one for us all. Chinook woke every few hours whimpering. I thought at first he was thirsty or hungry but really he just wanted to snuggle with us.

Montana.

Wolf pups grow extremely fast. They need to because by fall a wild pack expects the pups to relocate with them in search of food. At seven months old, they have acquired enough knowledge and skill to assist with the pack hunt, and by ten months they are virtually indistinguishable from the adults. Only their immature hunting strategies betray their age.

Our pups were definitely keeping up with the normal growth pace. Their bellies bulged after consuming one-and-a-half pounds of raw meat and as much dry dog food as they wanted. When they fed, they ravenously attacked the dish. There was no pacified sharing between the two when food was involved. It was each pup for himself. I was surprised by their aggressiveness but I should not have been; in the wild, timid wolves go hungry. Despite Montana's smaller

Chinook.

size, weighing only five pounds to Chinook's nine, he was a little pistol, ready to take on the world.

One would think having the pups in our home would have allowed Bear to fulfill her maternal instinct. But the opposite occurred. She shunned them. She showed no motherly desire to fuss over them but instead growled and snapped whenever they got too close. She appeared genuinely irritated by them, which confused the pups, because they saw her as a surrogate wolf mother. They would greet her and want to play just as they would with a pack member. They did not understand her aggravation. They tried poking their muzzles around her mouth to encourage her to regurgitate partially digested food, an action called "lick-up." This behavior only caused her to pull her lips back and bare her teeth. They quickly recoiled into submissive postures.

"Bear, don't be so mean," I scolded. But despite my wish for Bear to dote over them, she remained firm in her dislike. I was baffled.

I had thought Bear's close chromosome configuration to wolves would stir her to explore their similarities. In the 1980s, humans went crazy for baby apes; there was something undeniably familiar and cute about chimpanzees, which share 98 percent of our genetic makeup. I thought Bear might feel the same magnetism.

Montana and Chinook play in the backyard.

The wolf is embedded in every dog, and for breeds like the Akita—so similar to wolves with muscular frames, dense fur undercoat, instincts to hunt bears and dominate other dogs—surely they are not that far removed. Certainly if Bear had been a Chihuahua, it would be a stretch to see the link between her and a wolf, but that was not the case.

My time with the pups was going by too quickly. The pups spent every afternoon in the outside kennel next to the house. As I watched from a distance, their play turned serious. It was preparing them for pack life. One of their favorite games was ambushing each other. They were also learning dominance and stealth. While Montana took his naps, Chinook would inevitably silently trail him and then pounce. This quiet, delayed approach is vital for stalking prey in the wild.

When the two were playing—and they played with anything, sticks, bones, leaves, you name it—Chinook usually wanted whatever Montana had chosen to gnaw on. He needed to interact more than Montana desired a playmate. And as the days passed, Montana developed as a lone wolf, choosing solitude over companionship, thus contradicting what I believed inherent in a pack animal.

On June 12th the pups made their premier appearance at the zoo. As I spoke to visitors about wolf conservation, they charmed the crowd with their antics, like chasing a springing grasshopper and demolishing the flowerpots that skirted the amphitheater stage. They were intrigued by everything and anything, which proved somewhat painful in Chinook's case. At first I paid little attention as people pointed, laughed and snapped photos, but the ruckus continued so I turned to look. There was Chinook, squirming and whimpering as he tried to free himself from the wooden rainforest cut-out he had gotten stuck in. He did make one cute chubby monkey. I pried him loose and was rewarded with a slobbery face lick. Since he had already upstaged me, it was a good time to end the talk. As I tucked one pup under each arm, a woman from the crowd expressed how she envied me. I smiled and admitted how very lucky I felt.

With the wolf pups a part of my daily life and the pack accepting me into their world, I thought the summer could not get any better. But it did. Amanda, now fifteen years old, was coming to visit. I could not wait to introduce my daughter to my wolf family. I was giddy with excitement.

The forty-eight hours after I found out seemed to drag. Even interacting with the animals did not keep my mind from wandering back to Amanda. But caring for the wolf pups had to come first, even before preparing for my precious house guest.

As part of the pups' health regime, they were weighed twice a week. The week of Amanda's arrival, the weight gap between them was widening; Chinook was almost twice as heavy. Montana's lack of weight gain plus his disinterest in food worried me. Since Shadow's death, I had become paranoid about losing another wolf to parvovirus. So when either pup showed the slightest behavioral change, I took it seriously. We became diligent, almost fanatical about their vaccines. Since wolves are highly susceptible to this deadly virus, we put the pups on the six-, nine-, and twelve-week-old injection series. We were taking no chances.

Dale and I concluded that Montana's loss of appetite could be something altogether unrelated, like the suffocating 97-degree temperatures. If in fact heat was to blame, then the plastic wading pool I put in their cage the next day would hopefully help them cope.

The water seemed to fascinate them. They quickly discovered the fun of chasing each other through the pool and awkwardly wriggling out the other side. Their aquatic tag would go on for several long minutes until exhaustion made them collapse spread eagle on the bottom with just their little heads bobbing above the water. The pool seemed to cool them down; however, it also created a rather large mud hole that they found equally amusing. They would slosh through it, then run to me and put their soggy paws all over my legs.

Finally the big day arrived and my waiting was over. Before leaving for the airport that afternoon I checked myself in the mirror more than once. I also devoted extra time to my hair. Dale thought it quite silly that I would put so much work into my appearance for my daughter. He always thought I looked great and did not understand my insecurity, or my need to score higher in every category than Amanda's stepmother. He was such a guy. Besides, I knew I had aged in the past two years so I needed to do all I could so Amanda wouldn't notice.

When the arrival of Toronto Flight #893 was announced over the airport loudspeaker, I focused on the passenger gate. There, I saw her squeeze past an older couple and walk toward us. I could not wait for the electronic doors to fully open before I rushed forward. I hugged and kissed her.

"I love you, sweetie. My goodness, you're so grown-up," I said.

"Love you, too, Mom," her soft voice replied. She seemed a bit embarrassed by my emotional outburst, so I pulled back and stared into her blue eyes. During our time apart, she had blossomed into a slender, bronzed, five-foot-tall young woman. Her shimmering, chestnut hair spilled over her tanned shoulders, and I realized I had been absent when she left her childhood behind. I hoped the closeness we once shared would still hold true. I cracked some silly joke, my way of dealing with nervousness, and her sunny smile reassured me my baby was still inside that mature body.

On the drive back home I chattered on like a chipmunk. I wanted to avoid any uncomfortable silence. I wanted her visit to be great, with no uneasiness. Whether that could be accomplished was yet to be seen. Dale played chauffeur and only occasionally interjected a question or two. Did she find tenth grade difficult? How was her pot-bellied pig doing? Did she have a boyfriend? Most of his questions were readily answered, except the last one. That one made her blush, and she smiled and simply shrugged her shoulders.

Within a short time our conversation turned to the wolves. Amanda wanted to see them as much as I wanted to show them to her, but since it would be dark by the time we finished dinner and got her unpacked, we decided to wait until the following day.

I was confident that Amanda's respect for animals, combined with her quiet, cautious demeanor, would work in her favor when she met the pack. Plus, I would be right next to her the entire time.

I woke early the next morning eager to fuss over Amanda and make her breakfast. But to my disappointment, all she wanted was a glass of juice. So while we discussed our day at the zoo, I put away the eggs, bacon, Fruit Loops, and muffins. Plainly I had to learn that she now had a young woman's appetite. Which seemed like no appetite at all.

As we walked along the zoo pathway, I kept staring at Amanda. I studied every curve of her face to see if she still resembled me or not. She spoke modestly but with conviction on animals and animal issues. I felt so proud.

When we approached Wolf Woods, the pack was searching for the remains of the meat Tom had thrown them earlier. It took just a few words of greeting for the six wolves to rush to the fence to meet us. Their tails were high and wagging, and Tina was the first to whimper her welcome. Amanda's face lit up. One by one I introduced each wolf to her and her to them.

"Do you want to go in with them?" I asked.

"No, that's okay, Mom," she replied.

"What, are you sure?" I asked, shocked that she would pass up such a unique experience.

"No, really, Mom, it's okay. I'll just watch them from out here," she answered.

I was stunned by her answer but appreciated her desire to take it slow. After all, going in with a pack of wolves can be a scary thing. When I was her age I had far from a brave heart.

Amanda during her visit.

We sat on the bench in front of the wolves and enjoyed just watching them. I glanced at Amanda, then at the wolves. My heart swelled with love and pride.

Throughout Amanda's stay she got comfortable with the pack but never ventured beyond the safety of the bench. She was quite content to observe them through the mesh wire.

Treasured moments seem to speed by at the rate of a hummingbird's wings, leaving us longing for more time. Before I was ready Amanda's visit was over. It felt like I had just said hello and now found myself at the airport saying goodbye. I clung to her, unwilling to let her go.

"I love you so much," I said as I hugged her.

She smiled and hugged me back. "Love you, Mom. Er err errrr," she replied by saying our customary hug noises. Ever since she was a small child those three sounds had been our special way of sending hugs to each other over the phone or in a letter.

"Okay, that's it. I'm not letting you go. I'll tell your dad your flight was canceled, and there won't be another one for six months." I was serious.

"Oh, Mom, you're such a guppy."

"I'm not a guppy." We did our best impersonations of Flounder from *The Little Mermaid* and broke up laughing.

The passengers began to filter through the boarding gate and I felt frantic, realizing our time was up. My eyes welled up again as I crumpled the soggy tissue in my hand.

Dale led me to the windows. For the next twenty minutes I stared blankly at her plane, thinking of how much of her life I had missed. Dale held me close as we watched the plane taxi down the runway and lift off. She was gone. For how long this time?

It was the end of June and several days since Amanda's leaving when I got back to the socializing schedule for the pups. They were old enough now to try them on a leash. And as expected, the rope and collar became an exciting new toy. They wrestled the rope to the ground and when convinced their "prey" was dead, they let me hang their trophy kills around their necks. With the wolves on leashes, I could take them out into the yard without worrying about them running off. Yet I certainly had no plans to train them like dogs. You can lead a dog on a leash, but a wolf on a leash leads you.

The Fourth of July weekend came and went. The continuous firecrackers exploding around the zoo's periphery eventually ceased, allowing the jumpy animals to finally relax. The male white-handed gibbon, Rocket, stopped his incessant territorial hooting; the bears went back to playing with a barrel in their pool. Cappy the capybara eventually left the security of his pond to retreat to the barn for his evening meal of fresh fruits, vegetables, and dry feed.

The end of the holiday weekend marked the end of the summer's rich emerald grasses. Sprawling lawns of ochre crabgrass were everywhere. The pups' weight and height also changed. They were now closely matched. Both now had the black-tipped guard hairs one third of the way down from the base of their tails. These hairs cover the dorsal tail gland. It is theorized that the secretion from this gland is rubbed onto the roof of the den entrance by pack members to claim it. The Heritage Pack did not typically investigate this spot on one another. Aside from the pups' weight and height similarities, a major difference between the two still existed—Chinook's lighter coat streaked with ash-gray. Fur color was the only way to distinguish between the two wolves.

Even though they were physically changing, one thing remained unchanged—how much they enjoyed their evening walks around the zoo grounds. Wolves are crepuscular animals, which means they are most active when the light is fading. Our walks allowed them time to experience new sights and sounds, although the walks consisted of more resting than walking. The pups would lie either beside me or on top of my legs. They loved to touch and be touched. And their affectionate wolf kisses were always rewarded with a hug. During our walks, their personalities were evident. Montana maintained his independent side and required less of my attention, while Chinook always solicited more petting from me.

As more and more of my days were spent with the pups, a complete trust evolved. I could not imagine ever being afraid of them even once they became adults. But this was new territory for me, so I could only speculate.

Unfortunately, all the extra hours I devoted to the pups had taken me away from the pack. Evidence of my absence presented itself in late July with Cheyenne. She showed an indifference when I called to her from the gate. Even repeated calling did not stir her curiosity. Over time the wolves had taught me that my first explanations for their behavior were often wrong, and that many factors can influence a wolf's actions. On that particular day, snipe flies were fiercely attacking all the wolves' ears. They had been dealing with this constant irritation for hours, so when they had a moment's reprieve they chose to rest over greeting me.

Snipe flies are attracted to the same thing ticks and mosquitoes are attracted to—carbon dioxide. These pests find you by detecting your breath. I tried all the conventional fly products to give the wolves some relief, but they seemed to have little long-term effect on these carnivorous bugs. Dry ice inside a fly trap, however, seemed to be the best protection against these ear-munching insects. The ice gives off carbon dioxide as it evaporates, and the flies flock to it, expecting a meal, but are instead forever trapped at a mock dinner table.

The wolves' fly problem was so severe that I decided to do further research on it. I drafted a survey and forwarded it to 63 facilities in the United States and Canada that housed wolves during 1996. The questionnaire was designed to determine if their canines suffered to the same extent as the Heritage Pack, where Tina and Shilo suffered the most tissue loss.

Solo, front, shows ear damage from relentless snipe flies, summer 1996.

I hypothesized that the male hormone helps ward off fly infestation. The data I received from the surveys fell into four groups:

1) These facilities housed only female wolves. All those animals were affected equally by flies.
2) The next group responded that their male wolves had more infestation and greater tissue loss than the females.
3) These facilities also had both sexes and there was no significant difference in the level of infestation.
4) The final fifteen wolves were housed in facilities that were not impacted by flies whatsoever.

My study ended inconclusively, but it did begin a network of communication between our zoo and others in offering advice for combating these seasonal pests.

As a three-month birthday treat the pups were led into the center shift section for their first protected contact, with mesh wire providing a safe barrier between them and the adults. Full contact means no barriers, but that would come much later.

Both pups hugged my legs as we walked along the fence. All of a sudden the four adults ran up to the wire to greet their new pack members. Their excitement scared the pups, who pulled back on the leashes and clung to me. I sat on the grass, and they huddled in my lap. About eight feet separated us from the pack. The pups seemed content to watch the adults from that distance.

Cheyenne and Tina showed the most interest in the pups. They pressed their bodies against the fence and whined, wanting to get closer. Wolves can anticipate the behavior of possible social companions like pups. Tina and Cheyenne's non-threatening whining told Chinook to come closer and not be afraid. He understood the message and within thirty minutes, he left the safety of my lap, moved toward the fence, and rested near them, although not close enough for them to touch him. He was not that bold. Montana, the more nervous of the two, not surprisingly chose to lie far from the ruckus.

After two hours of varied interaction between the six wolves, it was time to take the pups back to the house. As I walked them past the duck lagoon, and out of sight of the pack, a chorus of howls swallowed the afternoon air. Then there was silence. The pack was listening for a reply to their social call. The pups turned and faced the sound. They seemed to know what was expected of them. Doing their best to mimic their new wolf family, they tilted their heads to the sky and answered with low yips followed by high-pitched howls. The boys were growing up.

Chinook, starting to turn a bit gray.

For the next several weeks, the pups spent their days next to Wolf Woods and their nights back at the house. It became clear that soon they would have to live outside permanently, since they were almost full-grown and were nearly expert at destroying our front porch.

Two days later the decision was made and the pups experienced nighttime at the zoo for the first time. I barely slept and woke early, not to the clanking of metal dishes being dragged around the porch but to silence. For me it was a dismal stillness, although our four cats and Bear were probably overjoyed that the rambunctious pair were gone.

The pups adjusted well to living outside and gradually began to lose their chubby puppy look. Montana, however, was still the proud owner of his fluffy baby fur, which is why I started to call him my "baby boy." Chinook once again surpassed Montana and graduated to a sleek adult coat that gave him a distinguished, regal look. Their appetites also grew; they now ate almost as much as the adults, which we expected since their activity level had increased.

Montana, bigger, but still the baby of the pack.

And their previous nervousness with the pack was replaced with enthusiasm. They would rush to the fence to greet Cheyenne, who was always ready to exchange licks with them. But at times Montana stayed back and chose to run and investigate the fence line alone instead of interacting with the others. I could not quite figure him out. Nonetheless, every day was a learning period for me as I watched each wolf find his place in pack life.

Chapter 6

Wolves Are Wild, Dogs Are Domestic

All the zoo animals were in agony in the sweltering August heat. There was no escape from the blistering sun. Even the waterfowl chose to rest under the veil of the aging willow instead of on the exposed pond. And the wolves' vain attempts to cool off consisted of finding and following tiny islands of shade around the enclosure. Because of the heat and biting flies, the wolves seemed easily provoked. It was not surprising when a fight broke out between Solo and Shilo.

It was not a serious clash, but Shilo still lost, as usual. We put her in the east side of the exhibit so her injured leg could heal. Of course, she hated being there alone and spent most of her time limping along the fence. To ease her loneliness and get her to stop pacing and rest her leg, on August 5th we decided to open the slide between her and the pups and allow all three together.

Initially she snarled and nipped their muzzles. She reminded me of Bear. After a few days, though, she welcomed their company. Their relationship seemed to work. Shilo did not pay too much attention to them, which suited Montana just fine, and she stoically tolerated Chinook's persistent face licking, which pacified him.

As the days passed, something unexpected played out between the pups and Shilo. During feeding sessions, Montana managed to keep Shilo well away from his food, just like Shadow had. I was not sure if it was because adult wolves often allow pups to eat first and often share food with them, or if in fact Shilo was deferring to the dominant animal.

August 15, 1996, saw another major event in the pups' lives. Early in the morning before the zoo opened, we leashed them and walked them into the adult exhibit for full contact. Shilo had been moved back in with the other adults a few days earlier, so finally the entire pack would interact. Cheyenne was the first to approach the pups and instantly took the role as their mother, staying by them the

Chinook stands in front of Cheyenne, and Montana demonstrates submissive behavior on the ground. Montana and Chinook were put in with the pack for an hour a day in August 1996.

entire time. When they ran, she ran. When they played, she was right in the middle, sharing their fun and exchanging friendly licks. The pups' presence piqued the attention of all four pack members, and in no time at all the six wolves were sprinting after one another, weaving around the shrubs and trees. Even Shilo was allowed to play and seemed to really enjoy the pups. Perhaps she had missed them in her past few solitary days. Whatever it was, we were glad to see her happy. She deserved it.

The only time their game of chase paused was when a pup got an urge for some human contact. They would rush up to us and we would stroke their heads or bellies, and once they were satisfied, they bolted off to rejoin the pack. This went on for over an hour and then it was time to take them back to their area. Cheyenne was clearly bothered by their departure and started to whimper, and the pups whimpered right back.

"It's okay, guys, we'll come back tomorrow," I promised as I led the pups away.

People are drawn to zoos for the animals. That is a given. But what is not so obvious is how zoos manage to slip in education. They hide the unpleasant "e" word with terms like interpretive talks, touch tables, and live presentations. These persuade visitors to keep coming back, not necessarily the idea of being educated. However, the line between education and entertainment can get blurry. Part of a zoo's mission is to educate its visitors, but they mostly want to be entertained. How can a facility accomplish both? It becomes a very tricky balancing act; in many ways zoos mirror the excitement and the pitfalls of circuses. Despite negative connotations linked with circuses—the animals are kept in cramped quarters, are forced to perform, are disciplined if they do not behave during the act, and seldom experience the pleasure of grass under their feet—the exhilaration of an up-close animal experience is hard to deny. The smell of popcorn and cotton candy along with sequenced costumes and colorful spotlights, and no metal barriers between the spectator and exotic animals are but a few of the reasons circuses have been so popular for so long.

The new-age zoos of today, sometimes called the modern ark, try to distance themselves from the circus stigma and classify themselves more as living museums. But both circuses and living museums share a common element. They are businesses and as a business zoos make decisions based on the bottom line in order to remain operational. In this era of more intense, more extreme entertainment, the public expects thrills, not just dry facts.

It has become increasingly more difficult for animal attractions to draw people to their doors simply by offering live exhibits. The public demands more for their money; they want a show. So zoos are caught between trying to entertain and trying to fulfill their goals of conservation through education. Try as we might, zoo facilities invariably fail either as educators or entertainers—at least smaller facilities with smaller budgets do. Most zoos do not fall under the umbrella of mega-million dollar facilities, but we all still strive to give the public what they want without compromising our integrity or our commitment to animals.

School presentation with naturalist Jim Fowler.

Following that rationale, Dale knew we could make a dramatic impression on our visitors by taking the wolves out and giving talks, while always keeping in mind the safety of the visitors and animals. Having a top predator stand inches from you can be a moving experience. Cheyenne was the perfect animal for the job. She was often used in our outreach programs to school auditoriums.

One distinct outing sticks out in my mind. We went to a small school just west of Grand Island. There we were joined by world renowned naturalist Jim Fowler in an Animal Planet presentation. As the principal stood at the podium and introduced his guests of honor, the children shuffled in their seats and jabbered excitedly. Up and down the aisles their giggles could be heard, and only when the room quieted down did Cheyenne and I emerge from the shadows of backstage. Everyone was spellbound. Their "oohs" and "aahs" were not new to Cheyenne's ears. As a creature of mystery, she had elicited that response many times before, and if not for the sound of her nails clicking on the wooden floor, one might think she was purely a vision.

The children in the front row, despite their teacher's pleading for them to sit down, rocked up on tiptoes and tried their best to reach up and touch Cheyenne. I marveled at Cheyenne's calmness in a room swirling with excitement. And even though everyone was there to admire her, her gaze was not on them but rather on something at the back of the room. I searched for what had caught her attention but I couldn't see a thing that would excite her. A human's ability to detect a moving object is far inferior compared to a wolf's. The humans in the room that day did not see what she saw, and yet her gaze gave everyone a rare opportunity

Cheyenne, calm and majestic, was the perfect wolf to bring to school presentations.

to experience the intensity of a wolf's stare. Teaching them about wolf conservation came easy after that.

I am a firm believer in the power of educating through the use of live animals. Not everyone supports that practice, I had learned six months earlier while attending a zoo conference in Minneapolis. Another conference delegate was dead set against using a wolf in such a way. Both of us were firm in our opinions and determined to convince the others at the conference why our way was the best. When this woman, representing her facility from South Dakota, did her school wolf talks, she took her dog. But I posed this question to her—would cheetah conservation be where it is today if Cathryn Hilker, feline trainer at the Cincinnati Zoo, had used her tabby cat during her presentations instead of her graceful and breathtakingly beautiful cheetah, Angel?

Hilker greatly benefited cheetah conservation because using the real thing is more dynamic and moving. I have seen cheetahs in the wild, but being within touching distance of Angel bolstered my support for the world's fastest cat. I knew using Cheyenne when I taught about wolf conservation could convert a mere spectator into an advocate. When children looked into her eyes, they felt an attachment to the animal. That emotion stirs people to care and act.

The passion we noticed in the schools is the same passion that catapulted the giant panda to the top of the environmental issues in the early 1980s. Similarly, when the movie *Gorillas in the Mist* came out in the late '80s, the Mountain gorilla took center stage. The spotlight shifted to African lions, warthogs, and meerkats when children craved anything and everything to do with *The Lion King* in the '90s. And most recently the GEICO ads of the twenty-first century ignited interest in gecko lizards.

Once people are introduced to an animal in positive light, that species is often popularized to the point of a national or international craze—being well known and beloved, they stand a better chance in the wild. However, those species that do not get extra media attention, or those considered not-so-adorable, have fewer vocal advocates and receive little to no support. But they are in need of the same support. How will they survive the impact of human encroachment with no one in their corner? The dismal reality is, they probably will not.

Zoo animals are ambassadors for their wild populations. In some cases, the last remaining specimens of a species are entirely in zoos; no longer existing in the wild. Without these select animals, it becomes an insurmountable task to educate people about all species and their individual plights. I was not able to change the woman's opinion that day in Minneapolis, but I am convinced I have changed some adults' and children's attitudes toward wolves with Cheyenne's help.

When a live animal evokes such a depth of passion, there can be drawbacks. Such was the case during one of my afternoon walks with Montana. Because of the pups' size and strength, I could no longer walk both at the same time. Their exercise walks were rotated and on that Labor Day weekend afternoon, it was Montana's turn. We were on the path next to the lagoon when Montana homed in on some duck droppings. He slumped to his knees and rolled his face in the green slime. *Lovely*, I thought. As he was enjoying his fecal facial, a family of three saw him and hurried over. The young boy reached us first. He tried to touch Montana, but I quickly moved between him and the wolf. I could tell he was put off by my interference. Disappointed, he took a step back.

Staring beyond me, he said, "Whoa … is he ever cool! I want one as a pet."

I could feel myself tense up. I understood his reaction and although I doubted he was thinking much beyond how "cool" Montana was, I hoped the experience would someday convert into something much deeper thereby avail wolves.

Nevertheless, the boy's comment shot my mind back to an appalling story I once heard about a California man. The man bought a wolf named Bart for a pet because he thought it made him look tough. But Bart was not a dog, nor did he understand what the man expected from him. The man thought because Bart looked so much like a dog, he should act like one. That he could be tied up and obedient, and if not, then the man would beat it into him with a crowbar. That is when the horror began for Bart. Sadly, he never learned those lessons and was left tortured and with no will to live. Bart never knew the pleasure of body rubbing another wolf, chasing or being chased by a fellow pack member, sleeping huddled close with a pack, or joining in the joy of howling. He did not live a wolf's life but a life of physical and mental suffering with each step he took as he circled the same tree day after day, leaving the ground beneath him worn away.

Bart's image and the images of all wolves long gone were so strong in my mind that I stooped down next to Montana and wrapped my arms around his neck ignoring the caked-on duck dung.

"This hug's for you, Bart," I said softly. It occurred to me that I was trying to expose people to the wonders of wildlife and at the same time I was dispelling their fears and giving the impression that wolves could be a house pet. I overwhelmed the boy with my speech on wolves versus dogs, coming off, I'm sure, like the keeper from hell.

Most theories suggest that all breeds of dogs descended from the gray wolf, while only some breeds (the spitz breeds) still physically resemble wolves. Wolves and dogs underwent different selection pressures; while some might have acquired similar responses to situations, for the most part they employ different problem-solving strategies when confronted with a task.

According to Ben Ginsburg of the University of Chicago, "When you introduce a dog to a bunch of wolves, you might expect the wolves to kill it. But in fact they treat it as a juvenile. If you want a real thumbnail sketch of the difference between wolves and dogs, it is that the wolf is the adult form. The dog is a juvenile wolf. The wolf demands dignity and respect, the dog you treat as a child."

I finished my speech to the little boy with, "Wolves are not and should not be viewed as pets." I looked down at the boy and at once knew I had not gotten through. He was so absorbed in Montana that I am sure all he heard was unintelligible adult garble. Nonetheless I hoped his parents at least understood what I was saying, since conservation was the media message of the decade. Looking at them watch Montana, I immediately flipped from serious lecturer to mutual admirer. I could not fault them for ignoring my admonitions. After all, who would be anything but thrilled or overcome with awe to have a wolf inches from them. It's so rare and special. And the grandeur of a wolf never changes.

I walked away with Montana, aware that by showcasing the animal in a way that promotes the perception that they are tame and easily adaptable to living as pets, our educational message was failing. We needed to make the distinction clear: wolves are wild, dogs are domestic.

Webster's Dictionary defines "domestic" as "trained, or living in a tamed condition." The definition of "wild" is "not easily controlled, and living or growing in its natural state." There needs to be a third classification for animals like Montana: "socialized." That is where the Heritage wolves and most other zoo animals would fall, midway between both definitions.

Throughout my years of working in zoos, I have seen and heard of numerous incidents of people buying an exotic animal as a pet and wanting to get rid of it soon after. They aren't prepared to care for it over its entire lifetime. This trend is part of our culture's infamous addiction to impulse buying.

Grievously, it is not limited to clothing or toys but extends to living animals. Organizations like the ASPCA, the Humane Society, and even reputable pet stores restrict the sale or adoption of specific animals at certain times of the year—bunnies and chicks at Easter, black cats before Halloween, and puppies and kittens during the Christmas season, all in the hopes of curbing people's impulsive urges to buy a warm and fuzzy friend without thinking it through.

We have an insatiable hunger for things, and usually if we lose interest in these objects, they can be easily tossed to the back of the closet or garage. But it's not so easy with an animal. They are not disposable. At that point, zoos, sanctuaries, and animal shelters are called. They are asked to take these unwanted animals, anything from turtles to tigers.

One of the troubling aspects about these calls is the callers honestly believe they are the first to ever want to ditch their pet. Zoos get hundreds of calls a year, and the somber reality is, most do not have the space or financial means to accept anywhere close to every animal in need of a new home. It is a disturbing situation. These facilities hate to say no to these requests, because then what will happen to the poor unwanted pets?

Desperate for a solution, some people just release the animal into the nearest field. They drop it off on some remote country road, toss it into the nearest creek, or kill it. None of these options have the animal's or the ecosystem's best interests at heart. Indiscriminately releasing animals into the wild is precisely how many non-indigenous species have been introduced into areas. Ed Bangs, wolf recovery team leader for the U.S. Fish and Wildlife Service, laments the ritual, "It's extremely cruel to think you can turn a wolf or hybrid loose and assume they will become a wild animal. They never can return to the wild." The animals almost always starve to death, are shot by ranchers, or are run over by vehicles.

These solutions do not benefit the animals. Nor does human responsibility does evaporate once the animal is out of sight. And though the unwanted house guest is gone, it is not without disastrous results. 🐾

Chapter 7

Solo's Reign

Left to right: Montana, Tina, Cheyenne, and Solo on her summit, reigning over the pack.

Most of the members of a pack are extended family—the alpha pair, their offspring, and many times, the alpha pair's siblings. Because of this makeup, a wild wolf pack has a strong connection to one another, whereas a captive pack usually consists of unrelated individuals and has looser ties. Within the Heritage Pack, instead of one unified family three separate teams emerged: Solo and Tina, Montana and Chinook, and Shilo and Cheyenne.

A captive pack also does not need to hunt for their food, which would strengthen a pack's bonds in the wild. When this cooperative hunting is absent, the links between pack members are weakened.

These two factors could explain why the Heritage Pack appeared to have a slack association with one another and seemed to lack stability. Much of this was due to Shilo's refusal to resign herself to her omega position within the group. If she could have successfully established dominance or accepted her low rank, then the pack would have been more cohesive. But she did neither, which created conflicts that escalated to physically dangerous levels.

Normally a highly-developed sense of pack hierarchy allows the wolves to settle their differences with little or no disruption to the pack as a whole. Solo fiercely communicated these well-defined rules of conduct by reigning with an iron paw. One might compare her to Yellowstone wolf Number 40, who was the matriarch of the Druid Peak Pack. Number 40 rarely tolerated any other female, but was especially aggressive toward her sister Number 42, nicknamed the Cinderella wolf. Although she was not Solo's sister, Shilo suffered similarly under the Heritage Pack's matriarch.

An upbeat voice on the radio announced, "Don't forget to turn your clocks back one hour before going to bed tonight."

"Yeah, right. As if that's the most important thing on my mind today. Boy, is that guy's voice irritating," I complained to Bear. "Or maybe it's just me. I haven't had enough caffeine yet." She tilted her head and stared up at me as I emptied the remainder of the coffee pot into my thermos.

"Well, wish me luck, I'll see you later." I kissed her face and left the house.

Even with the bustle of activity surrounding many of the animals, the zoo had a soothing affect at 7 a.m. in the morning. The mallards vigorously splashed in the lagoon, determined to saturate every one of their feathers before the cold weather froze their pond. The swans matched the ducks' enthusiasm in their own creative water waltz. They rose midway out of the water and madly fanned their wings, as if trying to lift off while the pond held tight to their feet. They repeated this sequence several times before gliding off side by side to the middle of the lagoon.

Chinook, the alpha male.

The ring-tailed lemurs stayed huddled together with their tails wrapped around one another, not yet ready to greet the day. Bonnie and Nikita, our pair of black bears, ambled around the perimeter of their exhibit while always checking for their keeper's feed cart. The male ostrich lay on the sand swaying his head and huge wings back and forth like large palm fronds. And of course, the wolves serenaded all of the zoos' residents with their howls.

I could hear the wolves as I hooked my radio on my back pocket. I tried to figure out how many were howling. This would give me some indication if they were all okay. Although their howls sounded similar, each member had its own unique song, but I still could not differentiate between them. I had to wait until I got to Wolf Woods to evaluate everyone's condition.

That morning as I headed down the path to Wolf Woods, I felt that familiar dread sweep over me. During each new breeding season, I felt anxious just before my morning walk-abouts and that day was no different. I tried to hurry but my feet were unwilling to go any faster.

The wolves, I realized, had become my life. They were no longer just zoo animals that I was in charge of—they were my children. When I woke up, they were the first thing in my mind. As I fell asleep, they were in my thoughts. When the weather changed from hot to cold, I worried how each was coping. I looked forward to their reactions when they got a special meat treat or a bizarre new ointment sprinkled on their grass to roll in. I photographed them constantly, wanting to preserve their beauty forever. And seldom did my conversations lack some mention of the wolves. They were woven into everything I did, how I felt and what I thought.

Wolf social ranking is not steadfast; with each passing season, a pack's structure can fluctuate. Members can reach sexual maturity or old age, become wounded or sick, or shift alliances with other pack members. These things impact each member's standing. And as the mercury falls and daylight hours shrink, the wolves are propelled into perpetual motion. They leap from lazy canines of summer to creatures of heightened awareness and fixed purpose.

Animals are influenced by decreased or increased photoperiod. Photoperiod is the duration an organism is exposed to daylight. Fewer hours of light cause monarch butterflies to flutter south to Mexico, flocks of geese to undertake their arduous flight from their nesting sites on the tundra to the warmth of the Gulf, and white-tail deer to rub the velvet off their antlers as their testosterone levels rise. Decreased photoperiod is also what provokes aggressive challenges among wolf pack members.

As I neared their exhibit, Montana was squatting by the juniper bush while further away Chinook had his hind leg raised, indicating dominance. The pack appeared relaxed. Each member was busy with its own doings. After greeting me at the fence, Tina intimidated Solo into exposing her belly. It was highly irregular for Tina to try to displace her sister from the alpha

Montana, with his captivating stare.

Cheyenne instigates playtime with Tina while Solo stretches nearby.

position. A new breeding season sometimes brings a new alpha wolf, or at least competitors. For the most part the wolves were more amiable than I expected. I stayed and watched them for longer than I should have, putting off the rest of my work, but I always found it difficult to leave them once I was there. When I did finally leave, the pack was resting.

The Heritage Pack had also begun another ritual of the breeding season—scent-marking. Wild wolves scent-mark the perimeter of their range every one hundred yards; their scent lasts for weeks. Glands between the pads of their toes leave a scent when they scratch. Tina typically scratched the ground by her food before urinating next to it. A wolf uses all four paws to kick up dirt next to where it has relieved itself. This tells the next canine that passes that a wolf was there and to keep on moving.

Both wild and captive wolf packs are typically led by a mature, decisive male, but since the Heritage Pack males were too young, the alpha leadership remained female. As for which one was leader, evidently that was up for grabs and Tina accepted the challenge.

Countless times in the following weeks, Tina continued her displays of dominance over her sister. It was becoming clear that Solo's Summit needed to be renamed. During this period Chinook would often come up behind Tina and sniff her perianal region, and whenever she urinated he would investigate to ascertain her readiness to mate, even though he was too young to breed. Nevertheless, he still chose to lie within four feet of her every time she slept, initiating an intimacy between the two.

Once snow blanketed Wolf Woods, the pack settled into their new roles. Tina, at least temporarily, held the alpha position, and Solo reluctantly took over as beta but vented her frustrations on both Cheyenne and Shilo. Every time Tina body-pressed her, Solo reeled around and ran toward either of the other two females, causing them to urinate on themselves. Meanwhile, Montana and Chinook remained uninvolved, spending much of their time cooperatively feeding on a recently donated road-kill deer that had ventured to the edge of the highway for the road salt.

With Tina as the new leader, there were fewer attacks within the family. None of the members sustained any bodily injuries. There were, of course, daily gestures to reestablish each member's position. Tina would stand with her tail high next to Solo, and Solo in turn would lick Tina's muzzle. The males knew when to lie on their side and raise a hind leg to expose their groins, and both Shilo and Cheyenne kept a close watch on Solo to know when to seek refuge inside the den.

The wolves' entire day was not spent trying to define their ranks. There were intervals of play as well. Even though Cheyenne was not the youngest pack member, she had the strongest spirit of play and often initiated games of tag. According to an old Russian proverb, "The wolf is kept fed by his feet." The wolf is a runner and a chaser, and it has four different gaits: walk, trot, jump, and gallop. The trot, clocked at 8 mph, is the most common pace.

Wolves' legs and feet are well designed for winter conditions. Their long legs and narrow chests make plunging through deep snow easy while their large paws can act as snowshoes keeping them on top of the snow's surface, which helps them keep pace when bringing down a kill.

It was pure delight watching Cheyenne race the pack through the snow in a match of "fox and goose," a game I played as a child. It was a winter version of tag. One person was the fox, the rest were geese, and everyone plodded through the snow after one another. The wolves did not know the game but played it nevertheless. Even Shilo, on the outer sphere of the game, participated. A wolf in snow is truly one of nature's artistic masterpieces.

It was early February 1997 when winter hit with full force, stirring up an internal storm within the pack. Solo had concealed her growing frustration as beta long enough and finally unleashed her pent-up aggression by ferociously attacking Shilo. She pinned Shilo against the fence and tore at her legs and groin.

It took three of us to separate them and then to kennel Shilo. We slowly approached Shilo's "critical distance," where the flight distance is overstepped and the animal feels cornered. We knew enough to expect her to react violently, and she did. She snapped at the bite stick over and over again until we were able to loop a catch strap around her neck and toss a blanket over her head to calm her down.

For several weeks Shilo was kept in the quarantine area while she healed. It was during this time we decided to have her spayed. Spaying an endangered species was not the progressive, conservation-oriented resolution we had hoped to find, and yet it was a necessary step. This would eliminate her estrous cycles and presumably alleviate the conflicts between her and Solo. It was a drastic decision, but all other means of keeping Shilo free from harm had been exhausted. Only time would tell if our decision was the right one.

While she was being quarantined, she was able to safely approach me without receiving one of Solo's famous floggings. This had also been true in the early days after the wolves first arrived at the zoo. Shilo could have safely approach me, but back then she was too wary to take that chance. And by the time she felt at ease with her area and with me, Solo had established dominance and intercepted Shilo's overtures toward me and other pack members. By then, if she chose to ignore Solo's superiority, it was at her own peril.

I hoped her time away from the pack might change things for her. We had shared seventeen months of friendship by this point, and still she remained aloof, not letting me touch her even to treat her wounds. She kept her distance, about a wolf's length, even when I brought her meals. She always waited until I stepped away from the dish before she ate. Cautious, suspicious the entire time. Her life with Solo had forced her to be constantly alert and ready to fight. I wanted to help her relax. I would need to let her set the pace. It was for her to decide how our relationship would evolve.

Every afternoon for the next ten days, I sat in the quarantine room with her, usually on one side while she curled up on the opposite side. I would either read a book or talk to her. Sometimes I would simply study her face and try to figure out what she was thinking. I followed her eyes and guessed what she wanted. I knew she trusted me when she allowed herself to sleep. When she rested her head on her paws and stared at me I felt like she was studying me. And when a loud noise outside caused her to raise her head completely off the floor, well, that was nervous tension.

On one particular afternoon I was convinced we were about to break through the tactile barrier. As I sat reading, from the corner of my eye I could see her move ever-so-cautiously toward me. She kept her body low to the floor and stretched her neck out to smell the bottom of my boots. I stayed motionless as she sniffed the

Shilo was separated from the rest of the pack while her wounds healed.

leather. She was about to move up to my leg when I made the mistake of repositioning my book so I could see her better, and that is all it took for her to retreat hastily back to her corner. She never tried to get that close again.

Her wounds healed quickly, which put a deadline on our intimate time together. Soon she would rejoin the pack. We never did touch, despite my hopes for that kind of relationship. Nonetheless, I still felt a deep emotional attachment to Shilo. We shared a kinship. She needed me to bring her food, keep her safe, and provide a calming voice in an often stressful environment. The other wolves required all these things as well, but with Shilo each element felt magnified. Our companionship, although different from the others, was unique because it was survival at its simplest.

Winter refused to leave peacefully that year, but eventually spring emerged. Notwithstanding Chinook's noble attempt at breeding with Tina months earlier, his sexual immaturity produced no litter in May, which did not surprise any of us. What was surprising to me, however, was Tina's approval of Chinook's courting, since I had predicted Montana's early independence was the sign of a pack leader.

Spring was exciting because it was a coming-out party for many of the zoo animals. Much of the tropical collection had been housed indoors for seemingly endless months, but rising temperatures finally freed them from their claustrophobic rooms and allowed their keepers to plan enrichment activities, which are imperative for captive animals. Regardless of the circumstances that brought the animal to a zoo, it is the zookeeper's responsibility to enrich the animal to reduce boredom and distress. Keepers' creative skills are often tested to find new ways to stimulate their animals. But sometimes, if you are lucky, the enrichment is provided with no human effort whatsoever. Just such a case occurred in early May.

With 200 scent receptors in its nose, the wolf's olfactory is its sharpest sense. Yet on this particular afternoon, none of the noses of Heritage Pack detected the approaching object of stimulation until it was within eyesight.

Swaggering along in front of her keeper was Loula Belle, the zoo's pot-bellied pig. Typical on pot-bellied pigs, her short stocky legs strained under the weight of her plump body. Her harness made deep depressions around her neck and belly, evidence of her obesity.

This was Loula Belle's debut stroll around the zoo. It also proved to be an unexpected break from the wolves' customary naps.

As she labored along the path, her bristled nose skimmed the ground in search of morsels of food. She was oblivious to the commotion she was causing only a few feet away inside the wolf exhibit. The wolves crowded the fence trying to reach this enticing prey. She would have been an ideal prey—slow moving, lacking dangerous antlers, and small enough for even the novice hunter to be successful.

They clamored over each other to get closest to the pig. Her grunts teased them as she strutted leisurely by. But just when the wolves felt she was within striking distance, she tricked them and steered off toward the petting paddock, leaving them staring in disbelief. How cruel of the keeper to take such a perfect quarry from their midst.

Loula Belle was long gone and well out of sight, and still the wolves kept looking in her direction, hoping she might return. After several long minutes they finally gave up and resumed their resting poses. But how could they sleep with their senses so aroused. It was as though they were out on the plains running with their wild ancestors hunting the great bison herds of long ago.

Loula Belle piques Cheyenne and Tina's interest as she walks with keeper Chris R.

Although pork does not tend to be a mainstay of a wolf's diet, Loula Belle certainly tempted their palates. For the remainder of the afternoon, the wolves remained alert. They would not give into sleep readily that day.

Predominately a wolf's diet is comprised of large ungulates (deer, moose, elk, and caribou) and, when these prey are not available, sometimes beaver. Although the wolves were attracted to the pig, it was not until Cheyenne was taken for a walk the following week that a natural food source sparked an undeniable interest.

Wolves detect prey via chance encounters and tracking, which involves sight, scent, and sound. It was a chance encounter that brought Cheyenne within a few feet of the zoo's herd of white-tailed deer one day. I always took the wolves—only Cheyenne, Montana, and Chinook were acclimated to a leash—on a designated route around the zoo grounds when we went for walks, and it usually bypassed exhibits that might stress or agitate the animals in their cages. However, that day I was unaware that the deer had been moved to another sector of the zoo while their yard was being graded. As we turned the corner, I saw the herd just past the capybara pond.

Immediately, the herd's dominant male pawed the ground, tilted his head downward, and snorted, while his harem bounded toward the back fence, their tails flashing an array of white warning flags. Viewing Cheyenne as a threat to his breeding stock, the buck stood his ground. Cheyenne jerked on the leash, straining to get closer. As she closed in, hunter and prey locked eyes in the "conversation of death," as wolf author Barry Lopez calls it. "It is a ceremonial exchange, the flesh of the hunted in exchange for respect for its spirit." Even though Cheyenne and the herd had lived their entire lives in captivity, they still inherently knew their role in the game of survival. There was no confusion as to who was the predator and who was the prey.

It took both hands and all my might, but I managed to pull Cheyenne away, defying her strong and rigid desire to stay right there. She was engaged in a hunt, and she probably expected me to distract the healthy male while she closed in on one of the younger does, but instead I forced her to end the chase. As the distance between Cheyenne and the herd increased, the deer gradually lowered their tails and returned to grazing, but Cheyenne kept spinning her head back around to watch them until the Commissary obstructed her view.

It was her initiation into stalking prey and a lesson in how difficult it is to hunt alone, especially when someone interferes. That afternoon was also more than her normal share of enrichment. 🐾

Chapter 8

The Pack's Fury

That March while Shilo was being spayed, the wolves were split into two groups. Montana, Cheyenne, and Shilo (once she recovered) were in the south side of Wolf Woods. Chinook, Tina, and Solo were put in the north side. This realignment worked well for the subsequent months and fighting became nonexistent, but it was always our intention for the separation to be temporary. So once the warmth of spring settled in, which subdued the wolves' aroused breeding impulses, we opened the shift gates and allowed the six animals back together. It was a happy moment but short lived.

Initially it went remarkably well, at least between Solo and Shilo. When the fighting did break out hours later, Shilo was actually left untouched. Solo and Tina were injured, and Cheyenne was driven into the den. I stood behind the fence frustrated and angry with myself. Clearly my efforts to mimic natural existence they would have had if living in the wild was amiss. I felt I was fighting as hard to make the pack dynamics work as Shilo was to reign as leader. Neither of us were winning our battles.

It was dusk, and there was just enough daylight left for me to go back and check on Cheyenne. To my disappointment, she remained hidden in the den. Tina came to the fence and I could see gashes on her face and front leg. Solo had similar scars. Dried blood was crusted to the fur on her ears and hind hock area. My only proof that Cheyenne was alive was the occasional bark that emitted from inside the darkened hole whenever she caught sight of either sister getting too close.

At one point Tina headed to the den opening and Chinook followed, but her daring dwindled and she turned back and settled on lying under the nearby maple.

To my amazement Shilo took no part in this bout but rather was off by herself on the south side. But she was not alone for long. Tina got up, and with Montana in tow, trotted over toward Shilo. Although it seemed clear Tina was ready to take on Shilo, for the next hour she instead body-slammed Solo, forcing Solo into submissive posturing. It was during this sibling conflict that Shilo ventured over to the north side. She crouched low, kept her tail tight between her legs, and managed to reach the other side without being detected. Cheyenne continued to bark when she saw any of them pass by. The day's light was fading, but I knew I had to stay and monitor the unfolding tension since I was the one responsible for the situation. Dale would have to eat alone that night.

After numerous Tina/Solo clashes, Solo appeared to be sick of being picked on, so she took out her frustration on Shilo. Shilo knew exactly what was coming. She ran for the tunnel den on the south side. Solo tried to bite Shilo but didn't get to her in time. Fortunately, Shilo had wedged her body inside the den, making it impossible for Solo's snapping teeth to reach her. Having failed her goal, Solo redirected her attention to finding food scraps around the enclosure.

As the day disappeared, so did the wolves' desire to fight. I eventually felt that I could leave them. They all found a spot to curl up and sleep. I hoped there would be no more fights that night, but I knew nighttime did not necessarily mean they would all be calmly sleeping.

I walked away and decided that it would be best if I did not separate the wolves for periods of time because of the recurring reintroduction challenges. Each member would keep reestablishing his or her position within the hierarchy. Either that or I needed to keep the animals in two separate groups permanently. That was the choice I had to make but it was one I resisted making. Why, I do not know. Maybe my own splintered family life made me loathe to break up my wolf family.

I skipped the morning meeting so I could get to the wolves and see how they had fared during the night.

"Let everyone be okay," I said to myself. Tina was the first to greet me at the fence. Then came Montana and Chinook. They seemed fine. Tina's eye had swollen shut but there were no new injuries. Solo was favoring her back leg but also had no new wounds. Where was Cheyenne? I could not see her. I called to her but got no response. I called again, and still nothing.

"Come on, Cheyenne, right about now I'd love to see that gorgeous stare of yours," I whispered. Then, after an agonizing few minutes, she nervously appeared at the den entrance. She was noticeably tense. Her eyes darted from one direction to the other searching for Tina and Solo. From where I was standing she appeared to have no external injuries. I felt relief and failure at the same time.

Next I focused on Shilo. How was she? Where was she? My stress level was spiking. Then I caught sight of her standing vigilantly next to the south side tunnel, and she was unharmed. I leaned against the fence and cried. The pack had made it through the night, but this could not go on. This was no way to house these wolves, and I had only myself to blame. I needed to ensure each and every animal was free from attack.

That summer's attendance proved to be a record high for the zoo because of all the new babies. Visitors crowded around the 4-year-old Asian elephant Nicholas to watch his afternoon bottle feedings. He was the first and only

Shilo, in the safety of the south side den.

Nicholas, Heritage Zoo's baby Asian elephant.

elephant to successfully survive hand-rearing at that time. Visitors also had the treat of seeing Nairobi and Savannah, the two African lion cubs, tussle in their outside yard. But it was the smallest baby that most enchanted the visitors with his antics—the adorable ring-tailed lemur, Roo.

Roo proved to be a handful because he loved to squeeze through the wires of his cage to hang off the nearby tree. Every day he played catch-me-if-you-can with his keeper. When she walked by, he looked innocent as a daisy sitting next to his mother. After she left, he would slip through the mesh and dangle from the branches, only to scurry back inside by the time she returned. With each passing day his escape technique became more and more challenging as his little body plumped up. Then one day his charades came to an abrupt end, leaving Roo quite baffled. The staff could only laugh as he tried in vain to overcome the obstacle of his own weight gain. His free-swinging days were over, and he would have to settle for fun inside the cage with the other lemurs.

Nairobi and Savannah, the two African lion cubs.

The wolves spent the long, hot summer in a semi-dormant state with few conflicts. Spaying Shilo seemed to have a positive outcome. She posed no threat to Solo's leadership and appeared to have finally resigned herself to the omega role. Or maybe Shilo was not harassed because Cheyenne was now sometimes the target of Solo's aggression. Either way, the pack showed signs of a stable grouping. This led me to believe that perhaps the family members were finally secure within their roles. For the first time the Heritage Pack had order, but would it remain or would the onset of fall's darker days disrupt the balance once more?

Throughout this time Shilo and I established a sneaky feeding maneuver. To get food to her I would casually walk by the den, which is where she tended to stay, and toss food inside the hole without Solo noticing. Our ritual worked well, but Shilo had to keep a watchful eye on me and be ready to seize the food before Solo caught sight. Our ability to communicate using energy and body language, no verbal cues, brought us closer as we communicated on an animal level.

One morning during my routine cleaning of the wolves' cage, and before the searing heat drove all the animals to curl up and sleep, a visitor stood by their cage and asked me a question. The woman was probably curious because I could move around the wolves' exhibit with minimal worry as the wolves carried on with their day. She asked, "Do they think of you as one of their pack?" If she had asked me that question two years earlier, my answer would have been an ill-informed yes. But hours and months of wolf observations made me pause before answering.

Since I was no wolf whisperer, my answer was purely conjecture. I know they accepted my presence, but where I fit in and if I held a position within the pack, only they knew. However I did think that certain aspects of my role as provider—bringing them food, nurturing an emotional and physical bond, and trying to maintain harmony—might have been recognized by the pack as important. Having said that, even though my car license plate at the time read "ALFA WLF," I did not for a minute believe I was. I had enough good sense and experience not to be that arrogant. I was just a scrawny human that the wolves allowed in their company. The woman received more information than she was looking for and flashed a bored, fake smile as she walked away. Maybe I was answering the question more for myself.

The mischievous lemur Roo, realizing he no longer fits through the wire.

Soon enough, the morning rush hour was making room for a familiar friend. Yellow school buses showed up in traffic as though emerging from hibernation. Canada geese honked their greetings as they flew overhead, and the maple tree inside Wolf Woods was halfway through changing its green costume to red. Autumn had rolled around again.

Fall was a busy time for the staff and the animals. The bears devoted much of their days to searching for morsels of food. The drive to bulk up for their winter sleep was not a matter of choice, but rather at nature's insistence. Bonnie and Nikita did not realize that as captive bears they did not need a yearly hibernation. A captive bear's daily ration of food altered that natural behavior. However, their instinct to pack on the pounds could not be ignored, so hour after hour both bears dug for grubs, uprooted plant material, and hollowed out various logs, all in the hopes of finding one more bit of protein to consume.

While the bears were busy foraging, the staff began adjusting many of the exhibits so the animals could contend with the subzero temperatures Nebraskan winters were famous for. Some of the species were caught and moved indoors, while others were given extra tarps and straw bales for protection against the wind.

In addition to our regular keeper duties, several hours of the day were allocated to preparing for the zoo's big fundraiser "Boo at the Zoo." The event was labor intensive but necessary in order to financially sustain the zoo throughout the winter off-season when the zoo's attendance dropped. Before the week-long Halloween event, the staff put in very long days and nights, and for the most part we did not object. It reminded us of childhood and we got to play dress-up. Every year the event got more impressive, and we hoped 1997 would break all the records. To add some fun to the work, the keepers proposed a contest. Each of us would take a section of the zoo and create a scary scene. At the end of the week they were judged, and the winner would go home with the Mystery Bag. Since we worked at a zoo and often a fellow keeper filled it, the Mystery Bag could contain something nasty or nice.

Initially a few subordinate pack members grumbled over the idea, feeling less than creative that year, but they were overruled once the betas Tom and Joel insisted. The challenge was set and the competition was on. We dispersed from the meeting eager (some more than others) to release our demonic imaginations. This was one time the staff did not act as a unified pack but disbanded to explore and claim areas of the zoo territory.

The seven-day event went off without a snag, and by the time the moon illuminated the night sky on October 24th, we had handed out close to 1,000 trick-or-treat bags, scared over 400 children in the Haunted Chamber, and gave 850 rides on the Zombie Express train. It was great fun, and the little goblins went home with a wide assortment of teeth-rotting taffy treats. As for the keeper contest, Chris won the Pooper Scooper Phantom award for her Wispy Apparition display. Chris was the bear and ratite keeper. She had a genuine talent when it came to working with crafts and woodcarvings. All the wood-lacquered fact plaques throughout the zoo were Chris' creations.

Chris R.,
bear and ratite keeper

After the ghoulish mood evaporated, zoo life went back to normal. Monday morning, I planned to savor my day off. A week of sixteen-hour days had worn me out. Plus, there was the added anxiety we felt for our animals and how the event had disrupted their sleep patterns and feeding routines.

Tom was my relief keeper on my days off and although he never outwardly admitted so, as a reptile enthusiast he probably did not like the carnivore rotation.

The zoo radio crackled next to me as I lounged on the living room couch.

"Sandra, this is Unit Three. Are you there?" Tom waited a beat then began to repeat himself.

"Yes, go ahead, Tom."

"Shilo's refusing to leave the den, do you think I should go in and check on her?" he asked.

"I'm sure she's fine. She's probably just trying to stay out of Solo's way."

"Okay, thanks ... 10-4," he signed off.

It had become almost customary for Shilo to escape to the den. It was her only remaining sanctuary. In the preceding weeks, the den had been where she spent most of her time—either inside or just at its entrance.

Shilo's hiding in the den was not much of an indicator that something was wrong, but her periodic barking that Tom had mentioned was. Barking is unusual in wolves and is almost always a signal of alarm or distress. A part of me believed she was fine, but another part nagged at me to get off the couch and check on her. My fatigue won out and I returned to my book.

Animals communicate loudly, if only we would listen. Their messages are clear through body posturing, facial expressions, a wide range of vocalizing, and even in how their hair lies on their bodies.

Shilo and Solo had been through this multiple times. As the scapegoat, Shilo's life was full of continual harassment from the others. She bore the brunt of the other wolves' frustrations. Sad as it was, that was her role within the pack and it included physical and mental stress caused by either Solo or Tina. They would act dominant and overpower her, and she would retreat to the den to live alone within the pack.

In the wild when a member of the pack is harried to this extent, the animal is often, if not always, physically forced to leave the pack and find its own territory. It is extremely dangerous for a lone wolf to search for new territory and a new mate. The animal must sneak through claimed tracts of land without being detected by the resident pack. If unsuccessful and he or she is found, the pack will attack with intense ferocity, often killing the intruder.

As a lone wolf, life is harsh. Without the help of other pack members to pull down a kill, food options also dwindle. A lone wolf becomes a scavenger or resorts to smaller food choices such as snakes, ground squirrels, birds, rabbits, and even berries. The ever-present danger of coming across other wolves keeps its senses alert. It is a stressful time but also a time when instinct strongly drives the wolf to pursue a mate, so it can begin life in a new pack. So, despite the risks, a lone wolf will place itself in a hazardous situation hoping to be strong enough or appealing enough to convince a wolf from an existing pack to follow it to a new region and a new lifelong coupling.

Before the wolves began harassing Shilo so mercilessly, Shilo and Tina had spent many peaceful moments together.

There is a strong possibility this would have been Shilo's fate had she been a wild wolf. She would have been pushed from the pack, as was happening to her in captivity, and would have followed the path of a lone female in search of a mate.

With my long weekend behind me, I woke rested and was excited to see the wolves. It had only been two days, but they were so much a part of my life that I needed an emotional fix. I bundled up and headed over.

It was not uncommon to get snow in October, and the night's storm had pounded the zoo with eight inches. I trudged through the snowdrifts with renewed energy. The first snow always made me feel refreshed. I reached Wolf Woods, and as expected, the wolves came running to the fence to greet me. Not all the wolves came and that too was expected. I worked my way around the perimeter of the exhibit calling Shilo's name.

"Here, girl. Come on, Shilo. Come and see me." It usually took several calls to coax her from the security of the den, but she always obliged and would eventually surface. She usually stood alert on the top of the den mound ready to rush back inside if need be. But this morning was different. I was already at the south end of the exhibit, and she still had not shown herself. Normally that would have worried me, but I was certain the heavy snow at the den entrance dulled the sound of my voice making it hard for her to hear me. I called out louder. By now I was positioned directly behind the den site and still no Shilo. Something was terribly wrong.

The snow became my enemy as I plodded through the drifts to get to the front of the exhibit. From there I would be able to peer into the den and see her sweet face looking back at me. But before I got there, my eyes were drawn to a heap just outside its opening. The mass was smeared in mud and snow. I moved closer, blinking repeatedly and believing the cold air was blurring my vision. But the cold had nothing to do with it. My stomach knotted and I had a sudden urge to vomit. I fumbled through layers of clothing to grab the radio off my back pocket. My hand shook uncontrollably, making the simple task of pressing a button tough.

"Seven to One. Seven to One," I called. "Shilo … Shilo's down." Not knowing if Dale received the transmission, I began to run toward the exhibit gate. The deep snow was no longer an issue as I sprinted to the gate in seconds. I was not sure why I was running. Did I think I could still save her if I was just quicker? Did I really believe I could do something for her? Tears surged down my cheeks.

"It can't be true, please don't let it be," I begged as I knelt down next to her, my tears turning to icy droplets as they fell on her body.

"I'm so, so sorry. Forgive me, girl. Forgive me," I pleaded. Her gruesome figure was more than I could cope with and I sobbed hysterically. I wanted to turn away but forced myself to look. I stroked her face and for a second lost myself in

Shilo, the omega wolf, was found dead in October 1997, after being attacked by the rest of the pack.

the realization that this was the first time I had ever touched her. Her fur felt soft under my fingers. I brushed the dirt away from her eyes then gently closed them. As my eyes traveled down her body they stopped at her chest. Was it moving? Yes. I was sure of it. "Come on, Shilo. Come back to me," I whispered. If I willed it hard enough. If I begged long enough maybe it would be true. But my imagination was just playing a cruel trick. There was no life left in her tortured body. I knew that. Her end had come hours before, during the cold darkness. While I was sleeping warm and safe in my bed, she was fighting with everything she had. Why had I not heard her cries for help? Why had I not felt her fear? Why had I not woken up in time to save her? I hated myself.

The pack gave us no trouble as Dale and I carried her body out of the exhibit. They were done with her. I desperately wanted to see some sign from any of the wolves that they felt some emptiness. I was not expecting such things from Tina and Solo, but I was sure Montana and Chinook would acknowledge what we were doing with their family member. But all they did was smell the spot where her rigid body had lain.

Why did the wolves feel no loss after the death of their pack member? Jim Brandenburg once wrote of a pack of arctic wolves visiting the body of a dead yearling wolf, "One by one they would sniff his body then curl up beside him." I wanted to see evidence of this compassion in the Heritage Pack, but there was none.

Tom arrived just as Dale was locking their gate. No words came to him. No words seemed adequate to express the sadness we were all feeling. He put his arm around me and offered to do my work that day. I said nothing, but nodded and turned to go. But something stopped me. How could I leave her? What kind of friend does that? I owed her so much more. Yet now our time together was over, and her final battle, although bravely fought, was one she could not win against the pack. I hugged her one last time and walked away hoping she was now in a place where she ruled as alpha.

My keeper notes broke from my normal concise, clinical tone when I later wrote of her death. "October 27, 1997: Shilo was found dead, seven feet from her safety zone. Countless puncture wounds to the back, neck, and groin, combined with an empty stomach, plus plummeting temperatures brought her to the end of her story. She died a tortured death, a testimony to the life she led. She did not live the long and happy life she so deserved."

Some say rank is plotted out within the first few weeks after birth. Others argue that it changes throughout a lifetime. No matter how it comes to be, the omega's life is guaranteed to be one of frequent mobbing and, at times, ruthless domination by superior wolves.

Shilo's death created a gap in the pack mechanism. In order for the mechanism to function as nature intended, the gap had to be refilled. If Solo had been the one to die, there certainly would be a significant reshuffling throughout the pack. The beta would not automatically rise to alpha. The younger wolves would seek to improve their status within the hierarchy as well, and they would be ready to assert themselves. So who would the pack now choose to suffer their wrath? Who would be the next omega? 🐾

Chapter 9

The Darkness Returns

When an animal that has touched your heart dies, and in Shilo's case it was a grisly death, you feel as though you will never escape the sorrow. And as a zookeeper, you question your ability to keep doing the work, or whether you want to, because the image of the slain becomes unbearable. You want to rip it from your mind but it keeps coming back.

For weeks after the tragedy (and even to this day), I was riddled with guilt. I stumbled through my work routine, breaking down and weeping every time I passed her cage. I kept seeing her lying there, cold and lifeless, reminding me that I was to blame. I thought about how she must have suffered and how, like dogs, when two wolves fight others are recruited to join in. She probably had no allies that night, just her against all the rest. How would I ever get that out of my head?

Not only was I mad at myself, but I was angry with the wolves. How could they do this to one of their own? I wanted to withhold my affection for them. I was bitter and wanted to punish them. But that would be vindictive, an exclusively human emotion.

Animals do not exhibit malice toward one another, or so they say, even though their actions toward Shilo would contradict that notion. Solo's retaliation against Shilo when Tina body-slammed her sister during her alpha reign would indicate that they also seek revenge. All of this made me question my previous beliefs. Why did a species with reverent regard to the family unit and their bond to one another kill one of their own? I needed answers.

I later concluded this could be an area in which wild and captive wolves differ. The bond of the pack in captivity is less unified, or maybe Shilo was never truly accepted as a pack member. She was, after all, always on the outer edge—always at the family home but never invited to come in.

As an animal lover, I have spent much of my free time enjoying nature's diversity, and I openly admit nothing stirs the soul like seeing a mother grizzly and her cubs off in the distance become larger and larger in your camera lens, or hearing the sound of crushing bone as a lioness gorges on a gazelle, or watching a bald eagle glide low over a salmon stream. It is amazing to see them move through their domain without hesitation, without wire barriers. Fences hinder their movement and alter their instinct to procreate.

My views on wild versus captive were again challenged one day just before the new school year began. A family stopped by the wolf cage and commented on how they hated to see animals in cages. At the time I thought it a naive, ridiculous comment. Certainly in an idyllic world, all animals would roam free to live and thrive, but our modern society is far from unblemished, so much so that for many species a captive world is their only remaining option.

If not captivity, then extinction. That was true for *Canis rufus*, the red wolf. In 1980 the U.S. Fish and Wildlife Service rounded up fewer than twenty red wolves to be placed in captivity for breeding. Currently 207 now live in various facilities across the United States and over 100 others have been released back into the wild.

After Shilo's death I rethought my position on captive animals. Perhaps for some captivity is not a plausible option. Zoos have existed since the middle of the nineteenth century, at least that is when we began to use the word to define exotic animals in captivity. In actuality historians claim that traces of the earliest zoos came from ancient Mesopotamia.

Admittedly zoos are an old institution and yet still experience failure in maintaining healthy, viable collections with clean genetic lines. Zoo history has been one of trial and error. The once common practice of removing animals from the wild in order to integrate pure blood lines or conserve an endangered species is no longer required since the industry has had great success in propagating the majority of their species. However, in some select cases of large felines, as well as new species being discovered by field researchers, it is still undertaken.

For many people their only opportunity to view and enjoy the beauty and richness of our planet's flora and fauna is at a zoo or wildlife park, so even though a percentage of our population may despise seeing an animal in a confined enclosure, the need still exists for such institutions. Unfortunately there is often a trade-off of the animal's freedom for the survival of the species overall.

As we try to preserve our few remaining wild places and diverse species, we must also concede the need for captive wild kingdoms. Both play a part in our past and our future.

Even the darkest days can have moments when the light filters in. Certainly Shilo's death eclipsed them all, but in mid-December a glimmer of light poked through. I finished up my keeper duties and decided to sit on the bench in front of Wolf Woods and watch the wolves. It was time for me to heal and to forgive the pack. I stayed outside their exhibit so they were less preoccupied with me and tended to display more normal pack behavior.

Tina and Chinook.

As I quietly observed, I noticed Tina body-rubbing Chinook. She seemed to be playing out a seductive sequence. First, she pranced around in front of him and then nuzzled his face. Between intervals of nuzzling his face, she would gently place her chin on his back. He returned her facial rubs and then moved to smell her from behind. Their courtship dance went on for quite some time. This is known as "pre-proestrus" or "active solicitation." As I witnessed the two tenderly strengthen their bond with one another, I wondered if the Heritage Pack was about to have its first alpha pair. I felt my lingering sadness replaced with joy as I thought of the possibility of future wolf pups.

Of all the seasons, and each one has its own beauty, I think winter is my favorite. My fondness probably started when I was growing up in Canada, where I had plenty of opportunity to toboggan down a snowy hill or skate in backyards because it seemed every home poured their own rink.

As I grew older and spent more time walking the nearby woods and bird watching, it was the solitude and quiet of the winter forest—disturbed only by the comforting whistle of the black-capped chickadee—that made me the happiest. I loved the feeling of being immersed in nature. There is a healing of the soul that occurs when you take a wintry walk and your footprints are the only thing disturbing the flawless canvas of freshly fallen snow. Dale and I often shared memorable walks around the zoo grounds early in the morning or late in the evening, well after the zoo was closed. Surrounded by nature's pristine snowy white, I felt that nothing could ruin my content peacefulness. That would change in the early days of the new year.

New Year's Eve festivities faded into memories, and the neighborhood homes that circled the zoo took on a drab look as their Christmas lights were gradually taken down and stored in cardboard boxes. But at Wolf Woods, the situation was worsening. As it was the height of the breeding season, fights among pack members had not diminished much since Shilo's death two months earlier. For Cheyenne, the pack's new appointed omega, today would be anything but ordinary.

Each labored step Tom took during his morning rounds caused the wafer-thin layer of ice, which had formed on the deep snow the night before, to crack and crumble under his weight. The simplest of tasks was exhausting due to the frigid weather. Locks were frozen shut, snowdrifts blocked gates from opening, and frozen water lines demanded he haul pails of water from one cage to the next. One pail of water became a second layer of ice as it spilled when Tom lost his footing.

As he neared the wolf exhibit, he heard barking. Tom had become accustomed to howls, whimpers, whines, and growls, but barking was rare and he knew exactly what it meant. He tried to run, but the deep snow slowed him down. He cursed the weather.

He could not make out at first what was happening. Four, no, five wolves were mashed together in a violent attack. The snapping of teeth, low guttural growls, and a wash of blood and hair on the crystallized snow sent chills down his back. This was no January shiver. This was a death chill.

"Oh no. Hey! Yoh!" he shouted while smashing his gloved hand against the cage, hoping to break the wolves' concentration. But nothing pulled them from their frenzied mission. Cheyenne was pinned mercilessly against the fence, flanked on both sides by Tina and Solo. Chinook and Montana paced directly behind them, waiting to replace the sisters. Patches of Cheyenne's fur punched through the wire. Her eyes were wild with fear. She snapped savagely at her attackers, but fatigue and the blood hemorrhaging from her body were bringing death closer and closer.

"Solo! Tina! Come here! Come here, girls. Over here, Chinook," Tom shouted. But they were not interested in Tom or his coaxing. By now, Erika, who had been checking the nearby owl cage, heard Tom's frantic calls and came running. The scene was terrifying. Solo and Tina were relentless, determined to kill Cheyenne. They took every opportunity to squeeze through the maze of battling bodies to rip and tear flesh from Cheyenne's body. Was it the taste of her blood they thirsted for, or proof they had won the dominance fight? Did they need the evidence of her lifeless body lying still on the ground? What was it that kept them going at her and at her?

The morning sun filtered through the red gingham curtains and cast a rosy glow on the kitchen wall. The intoxicating aroma of hazelnut floated up from my coffee cup. I kneaded Mouse's ears while she purred contently in my lap. I slid down in my chair and shut my eyes.

"Sandra, this is Tom, are you there?" he bellowed through the radio that sat on the counter. Mouse's claws dug into my thigh as I sat up, startled by the voice.

"Unit Three to Seven, are you there?" Tom repeated. I shoved Mouse from my lap and reached for the radio.

"Unit Seven to Unit Three, go ahead," I answered, trying not to be irritated by the invasion of my quiet time. I knew Tom would not bother me unless it was important.

"Sandra, Cheyenne's hurt. There's blood everywhere," quivered Tom's voice. My body stiffened as the words sank in.

"Oh, God, not again," I shouted, as a picture of Shilo raced through my brain. "10-4, Tom, we'll be right there."

I turned and yelled down the hallway, "Dale, quick, Cheyenne's been attacked."

"What? What's wrong?" he asked as he came out of the bedroom.

"I don't know exactly. Tom just said Cheyenne's bleeding." I started to shake.

"It'll be okay, Dorth," he reassured. With no time for further consoling, we yanked our coats off their hooks and headed across the road toward the zoo gate. It was not until we were jumping the creek that I realized neither of us had put our boots on.

As we reached Tom and Erika, I could see Cheyenne hopelessly trying to fend off vicious jaws. The sisters worked systematically to wear her down, and by now Cheyenne had been fighting for her life for over thirty minutes, maybe more, since Tom had no way of knowing when it had started. When one sister would tire, the other would take over. Even Chinook and Montana attacked with vicious, snapping jaws, ignoring that this was their beloved family member who had nurtured and played with them when they were frightened pups only sixteen months earlier. I had never seen this side of Chinook and Montana before. It was frightening and disgusting.

Time was crucial, so Dale told Tom to call the vet and to bring the van around. Erika and I grabbed the bite sticks that were leaning against the fence and entered the cage. It was evident Cheyenne was going into shock. If we did not get her out soon, she would have to be carried out like Shilo. Looking down at her ravaged body, I felt nauseated. The pain she must have been experiencing was beyond my comprehension. Chunks of torn tissue, shredded muscle, and exposed bone made me wonder how she could even be alive, let alone standing and defending herself.

We kept our backs to the door as we shuffled into position, putting ourselves between Cheyenne and the others. The secondary shift door was left cracked open in hopes Cheyenne would see an escape route and take it. But Tina quickly figured out our plan and headed toward the open door, blocking Cheyenne's retreat. I pushed Tina back with my stick, fully expecting her to snap at it, but she merely moved off to find another direction to come in. We realized we needed another course of action, but it was tough trying to discuss

An earlier moment of affection between Chinook, Montana, and Cheyenne.

Seeming to fall into the omega position, Cheyenne was attacked by the pack within months of Shilo's death.

anything in the midst of a wolf kill. I thought I would try something that always seemed to work in the past. As Erika stood as a shield for Cheyenne, I walked into the center of the wolf exhibit toward the shift doors. When I did my daily cleaning and unlocked the middle shift, they usually followed. They reveled in exploring the adjacent south side exhibit. Even though I doubted it would work today, I prayed anyway. Montana proved to be my hero; as soon as he saw me heading toward the gates, he ran over. Within minutes they were all around me. Cheyenne took just a second to realize now was her time to slip through the narrow opening.

"She's in! She's in!" yelled Erika.

Gratefully the plan worked, but Cheyenne's suffering was far from over. I quickened my pace back toward Erika but remembered not to run because that might trigger a predator/prey chase by the wolves. My 90-degree direction change left them puzzled since they were certain I was about to unlock their play area. They surrounded me as I made my way back to the gates. Chinook jumped up into my face and yanked strands of my hair with his teeth. *Oh, God, I'm next*, I thought as sweat built up under my clothing. Tina and Solo stayed uncomfortably close, right at my heels. I anticipated a bite to come at any minute. Witnessing the wolves' true wild nature scared the hell out of me, especially being sandwiched between them. But I was determined to do all I could to save Cheyenne's life. This time the omega would not be alone to face her fate.

Our next ordeal was getting Cheyenne loaded into the van. As I stood beside her battered body her legs began buckling beneath her. Every second counted.

"Tom, throw me her collar, quick," I hollered. He picked it up off the ground and tossed it ten feet, almost hitting me in the face. Approaching a wolf's mouth after such an attack is frightening, and I hesitated. Nevertheless I knew this was no time to be a coward. I cleared my mind and found some courage, just a little bit, but it was enough. As the metal chain closed in on her face, she reacted. Her jaws smashed down on it and with it, my hand. The throbbing was immediate. They say wolves' jaws have the crushing pressure of 1,500 pounds per square inch. Cheyenne easily could have broken every bone in my hand. Perhaps it was exhaustion, or maybe she recognized that I was a friend; whatever it was, all I suffered was minor swelling and bruising. On the second try Cheyenne accepted the chain with no resistance, and I led her into the back of the van. During the short but frantic trip to the vet's office, I sat next to her and stared at her mutilated body. Supposedly when a body is traumatized to such an extent, the body undergoes "stress analgesia," which is insensitivity to pain without the loss of consciousness. I hoped that was true for her sake.

Within minutes, we arrived at the clinic. The vet met us at the door with an injection of Telazol and in a matter of moments Cheyenne collapsed on the floor.

On the operating table, a closer look showed her tongue was no longer pink but gray, and her blood pressure was critically low. She was suspended between life and death. Further examination exposed extensive wounds over her entire body. The wolves had sunk their teeth into her rump and gouged her thigh muscle. It took thirty staples to close the huge laceration. She also had two deep gashes in her chest cavity and bruising throughout her back and hind area. The vet probed with his fingers to determine the depth of the bites in the chest and whether they had punctured her lungs. He shook his head in disbelief. He could feel her heart pounding against his fingers. It was truly amazing, but the tiny membrane lining the outside of each lung was still intact. She was incredibly lucky, if luck can describe a tortured body kept alive by a paper-thin membrane. The vet told us that had the membrane been torn, Cheyenne would have certainly died.

After five hours of anguish for all of us who worked so hard to save her, Cheyenne's surgery was over. Her intubation tube was removed, and she was given back to us. Since the veterinarian primarily treated small domestic animals, he preferred Cheyenne wake up back at the zoo rather than in his clinic.

When we finally returned with her, the grounds were vacant. Because she was still sedated we left her inside a kennel and placed the kennel inside the quarantine room. We walked away not knowing if we would ever see her mesmerizing gaze again.

No matter how hard we tried, neither Dale nor I could sleep. We lay in bed staring up at the ceiling and thinking about Cheyenne. We hoped she had enough fight left in her to recover.

It was after midnight when we decided to get up and go check on her. With the full moon's glow reflecting off the snow, we had no trouble finding the path to the Commissary. The still night air combined with the hazy moonlight filled me with a strange calmness. Oddly, my apprehension of what we might find vanished.

However, an instant later I suddenly lost that feeling as the quarantine door loomed before us. It seemed impenetrable as we stood in the darkness refusing to open it. I wished for some kind of a good omen. Soon enough one came from a hundred yards away. The wolves were howling. That was good enough for me. I was not looking for a burning bush.

The room was soot black and our eyes had trouble seeing, but like two beacons her amber eyes drew us to her.

"Thank God," I said as I hugged Dale. Finally our worries lifted. I hoped never again to go through what had happened these past twelve hours. I looked at Dale and his eyes were watering—his signature trait of feeling relief and joy. Cheyenne wobbled toward us and urinated on the floor. What a wonderful sight? I offered her some water, which she gulped down. It was obvious she wanted more, but her fluid and food intake would have to be gradual and rationed. She would have to wait for morning before getting anything else. I gave Cheyenne a quick neck hug before shutting the door and letting her rest.

By the time we got back into bed, there were only a few hours left before dawn. That was fine with me; I was convinced I would not be able to sleep anyway. But my emotional exhaustion pulled my body into a deep sleep and at 5 a.m. I awoke startled when Mouse's paw tapped my cheek.

Dale was already up and moving around when I woke. Usually he needed a good nudging to get out of bed, but his innate concern for animals often took precedence over his own needs. I admired that about him.

"Come on, Dorth, let's go," he yelled from the kitchen, obviously eager to check on Cheyenne.

"I'll be ready in a jiffy," I answered, equally concerned to see how she made out during the remainder of the night.

Cheyenne met us at the door, weak but standing. What a wonderful New Year's gift. For the balance of the morning I disinfected her room and replaced all her towels, which were soaked with blood from her drainage tubes. I rolled her antibiotic pill Cephalexin inside a meatball and gave it to her. She had no trouble gobbling up the snack. Then I concentrated on making her sleeping corner cozy. I knew I would appreciate warm blankets to curl up with if I was sick, so I threw several into the dryer to get them hot, then spread them on the floor for her. She went straight over and sniffed them, then tried to lie down but could not.

It was almost noon and she was still no closer to lying down than when I had bathed her earlier that morning. I agonized as I watched her stand over the warm blankets and stare down at them. It was obvious she wanted and needed to rest but was unable to get her body from the standing position to the lying position since her groin and leg staples had begun to tighten with each passing hour. Finally, after several attempts of circling the blankets to find a painless position to take, she accepted that one did not exist, and lowered her body in an amazingly gradual rate of descent. I wanted to applaud her accomplishment. If she were human most certainly she would have grimaced and moaned through that painful ordeal, but as a wolf she suffered silently.

For the rest of the day our time together was spent with her either laboriously trying to lie down or get up, or her standing while I bathed her chest wounds. I so wanted to erase Cheyenne's suffering, but could not, so instead I stroked her head and neck and tried to distract her with some pleasure. As the hours passed, an extraordinary closeness developed between us. When I washed her bruised and beaten body, she certainly could have moved away, or worse lashed out and

Cheyenne on the road to recovery.

bitten me, but instead she demonstrated a gentle tolerance. It was as though she understood I meant her no harm and only wanted to comfort her.

Midafternoon the following day, while I sat beside her on the floor reading and caressing her fur, a well-known sound sailed through the chilled air into the room. I glanced down at her to see if she heard it. I watched for some sign of recognition from her, but she gave nothing. The sound got louder and still her head did not move off the blankets. But then, as if commanded to react, her eyelids lifted ever so slightly, and her golden stare fixed itself on the opposite wall. The pack was howling. Were they howling for her? Calling to their lost family member? Helping to guide her home? My romantic side wanted to believe so, but my realistic side knew it was merely the pack responding to a distant siren. Sirens always set off a pack howl. Maybe Cheyenne knew they were not calling to her. That would explain why her mangled body showed so little interest in their eerie echoes.

It took weeks, but Cheyenne slowly recovered. During her absence from the pack, we permanently split the wolves into three independent groups: Cheyenne and Montana were together in the middle section of Wolf Woods; Solo and Yukon, a 20-year-old male who had been rescued from a deplorable zoo in New Jersey, occupied the south exhibit; Tina and Chinook were in the north side of Wolf Woods. These pairings eliminated squabbles and attacks.

The days Cheyenne and I spent together began a friendship similar to the one Shilo and I might have had if only we had had more time. Because Shilo was a much more timid wolf, our relationship took months to evolve, not hours like Cheyenne's and mine.

Even though 1998 began with the brutal attack on Cheyenne, the year would have far more to offer in the way of jubilation.

Yukon, a new rescue, and Solo in their independent grouping.

With Chinook now sexually mature and Tina in full estrus, the two continued to court. They flirted and both engaged in reciprocal nuzzling, scent-marking, genital investigation, and prancing. Throughout the month of February, the two were seen mating at least four times, so we were all optimistic for a possible wolf litter that spring.

When Cheyenne was put in with Montana, she showed an excitable, almost comical affection for him by jumping on and over him, licking his face and chasing around after him to the point that he seemed annoyed. And although they eventually settled on a mutual liking, Montana's attention tended to focus on Tina. He frequently tried to have physical contact with her through the fence, and when Chinook caught sight of this, he would run over and both males would exchange snarls and snapping of teeth. Montana eventually gave up, for the moment at least. Since only one pair in a pack breeds each year, Cheyenne and Montana would face imminent physical harm by the alpha pair if they were to attempt copulation. But that was a non-issue at Wolf Woods since the two pairs were separated by wire, and Montana was more interested in Tina than Cheyenne.

Although Cheyenne displayed estrus behavior as well, she underwent what is described in domestic dogs as "phantom pregnancy." This phantom pregnancy would have her produce milk at the same time as Tina, which would allow Cheyenne to act as surrogate mother if Tina, the dominant wolf, were to die. But as a subordinate, Cheyenne would be actively discouraged from breeding with Chinook, and if she did, her pups most likely would be killed.

There have been reported cases in which a lower ranking wolf secretively mated with another pack member, but it is rare and is quite risky for the covert paramours.

March came in like a lion with biting cold winds, but by the fourth day the winds had died down and a light, fleecy snow fell, making it a perfect winter wolf day. As I approached Wolf Woods to do my morning check, all but Montana were curled up with their noses buried in their ruffs. He was sprawled out on top of the dry straw inside the 10' by 10' wooden shelter. I guess he did not always prefer the life of a wolf. Within minutes all of them were hugging the fence for their morning greeting. There was no better way to start my day.

I returned two hours later with their breakfast of ground-up beef organs, which they rolled in before eating. Apparently it was so tasty Cheyenne even licked the extra off Montana's fur. Then both insisted on giving me a kiss, their mouths smelling of this goop. In moments like this, the wolves seemed to love nuzzling me. I had yet to truly appreciate it.

The following day when I went into the middle wolf area I felt a bit uneasy with Montana's attitude toward me. His behavior lately had been aggressive and agitated due to the season we were in and his inability to get to Tina. But to my

Chinook's over-enthusiastic greeting.

delight he interacted with me in his usual way sidling up for a belly rub and a kiss to his nose. Because I had little time to spare that day, my only attention to Chinook and Tina was a quick face scratch through the fence. Even if I had more time I probably would not have gone in; lately Chinook was becoming too excited around me and invariably tore at my clothing or jumped up, smashing me in the face. The experience was less than pleasant and my verbal no's did little to deter this strong, alpha male.

Solo and Yukon's pairing was going well. Right from the beginning Yukon established dominance, being older and having claimed the area first. He clearly showed Solo he was not intimidated by her. Within a short period of time they were seen resting near each other on the knoll and later trotting side by side along the fence line.

Throughout March, the three couples occupied their days differently. Tina and Chinook were immersed in courtship. Cheyenne and Montana devoted much of their time to digging a massive hole in the center of their enclosure. And Yukon and Solo continued to get to know one another. It was atypical to see Solo in the submissive, nervous role. Throughout her reign she had been fearless and things had gone as she dictated. Now she was getting a dose of the medicine she had treated Shilo to. During feeding Yukon ate first and only allowed Solo near the meat once he was done. He was a kinder leader though; he at least allowed Solo to eventually eat.

Chinook looks at Tina, who is lying in the den she chose.

As spring approached Tina spent more and more time walking the exhibit, her nose close to the ground, testing various ground areas by sniffing and pawing at them, and returning to some spots several times. Initially we thought she was tracking the scent of food, but as her routine consumed most of each day we knew it meant more. It was a methodical search for a den site and it alerted us to her pregnancy. Because the den location is important to the health of both the pups and the pack, she had to choose wisely. She had to find a place that was dry, warm, and unlikely to flood. Her chosen spot was northwest of Solo's Summit, with the den opening facing east.

Throughout the entire day and into the night on May 2nd, Tina was a no-show. She had entered her den early that morning and still had not surfaced when I left for home around 6 o'clock. Around 10 p.m. I walked back to the zoo to see if Tina might greet me at the fence. She did not.

By the following morning there was still no sign of her, so Dale and I prepared the camera equipment. We rigged a camera to the top of a remote control truck and the plan was to drive it down the hole to the den chamber and see what progress Tina was making. Like most well-laid plans, it did not work quite the way we had hoped. The truck proved poorly designed for rolling over uneven ground and toppled on its side within seconds of starting down the hole. We switched to plan b, a plan I was hoping we would not have to use.

"Okay, so you're ready to pull me out if I panic, right?" I said to Dale.

"Yes, hun," Dale assured me. "You just give the word and you'll be out of there as quick as a bull on red."

I stared down the tiny hole wondering why I offered to do this. What if Tina decided to come out while I was going in? Would she attack my face, or retreat deeper? I would find out soon enough.

I got down on my belly, and with my arms out in front holding the truck, I wormed my way down into the darkness. The flashlight attached to the side of the truck gave me enough of a beam to judge what direction to move this duct-taped disaster. Within minutes a 90-degree directional change in the path zapped out my light. I abandoned the truck right there and hollered to Dale to pull me out. The small opening left just one way to come back out. With ropes tied around my ankles, he dragged me to the surface.

"Holy Hanna, that's freaky down there," I said as I shook my hair and brushed the dirt off my face. "I need another flashlight to shine on the tunnel walls. I can't see a thing now that the truck is up against the east side."

"You're doing great," yelled Chris from outside the wolf exhibit, as she stood watching the TV monitor. She was in charge of letting me know where to position the truck in order to get the best picture of Tina.

"I can see her hip area," she yelled again. "If you can move the front of the truck either to the left, or shove the back of it more to the right, I think we'll have her in full view."

"Easy for her to say," I muttered to myself. I took a deep breath, flicked on the flashlight, and back down the hole I went. This time I took a stick in with me to give me extra length for pushing the truck further ahead. Determined to quickly put the truck in the perfect position so I could get out, I squeezed my body down and around the tunnel corner with record speed. My flashlight flooded the low tunnel walls, making it easy to spot the abandoned truck with its single beam propelling from its front. I used the stick to push against the back tires, which moved the front end to the left.

"I can see her face," Chris excitedly yelled to Dale, who then yelled down to me.

"Can you move the truck just a bit more to the left, Chris wants to know," Dale echoed to me.

I gave the truck one last nudge with the stick which rammed the toy up against the tunnel wall and an inch from the den cavern. But that did it, and on the screen Chris could see Tina and two pups cradled next to her belly.

However, that last ditch effort to position the camera had me underground one second too long and I started to panic.

"Pull me up. Pull me up!" I screamed at Dale. I could not even wait for him to start pulling on my ankle ropes before I shimmied my body backward out the hole. Surprised by the intensity of my own phobia, I sat on the ground taking deep gulps of air.

"Come look, quick!" Chris yelled. We knew there was a strong possibility we might lose the illumination from the pocket-sized flashlight that was providing the only light for the camera to bounce off Tina and her little ones. Dale and I ran to the exhibit gate. Once we got to the monitor, Chris pointed to the shadows on the screen and explained how Tina was lying and the indistinct dark forms that were her pups.

"This is so exciting! Way to go, Teen," I cheered and jumped up and down.

I spent the remainder of the afternoon glued to the monitor watching and listening to Tina and her pups. If she knew I was eavesdropping, I hoped she approved of my sharing in her motherhood.

At 4:30 p.m. the camera was pulled from the den after Tina objected to the intrusion by sinking her teeth into it. Immediately she and I began a tug-o'-war over the camera. After a few convincing "No, Tina!"s, she released her grip and I yanked the truck to the surface. The camera had suffered only minor injuries; it would be able to do battle with Tina another day.

Once all the cables and equipment were removed from the exhibit, Chinook returned to the area. He headed directly toward the den entrance to investigate our smells and ensure we had not disturbed his family below.

Two days after the pups' birth, I got on the phone with Gary at Wolf Park for specific coaching on pulling Tina's pups so they could become socialized wolves. I asked what mood changes I could expect from her once they were taken. He said she might behave in several different ways. She would do a lot of solo howling, appear quite depressed, require more affection from me to offset the loss, and may become destructive. Apparently one of his wolves totally demolished a wooden shelter. He also said she could very well be the type of animal that goes into the den, sees they are gone, and accepts it. So most likely, taking the pups would cause her intense emotional distress. It seemed cruel, but necessary.

At 7 o'clock that evening I went back to Wolf Woods to offer Tina some food. It had been three days since she had retreated down the hole, and in the wild pack members are responsible for bringing food to the nursing mother, so it was up to me to assume that role. Gary was certain she wouldn't leave the den when I called her, even though in the past she always came when called. But I would try anyway.

I tossed Chinook some meat to distract him and keep him away from the den entrance, as well as keep him from jumping all over me.

"Tina. Tina girl. Come here, Teen," my voiced trailed down the hole. "Tina, come on." Nothing happened. I almost decided Gary was right. Then just as I was about to turn away, a black nose poked out of the dimly lit, dusty hole.

"Hi, Teen. Good girl, Teen," I kept repeating as I rolled meat balls down the tunnel. She gulped them as fast as I tossed them. Slowly she ventured further from the security of the darkness to lick every morsel from the meat bowl. Once again Tina and I shared something exclusive. She had been the first to exchange a wolf kiss, now she trusted me to feed her after her exhausting achievement.

It was an amazing moment, as so many were with the wolves. I wondered how a once bashful, insecure little girl could end up in such a wonderful place with such magnificent creatures. Perhaps the answer is simple. If our hearts are open, incredible dreams can be realized.

One thing I have learned in life is that there is always balance. Life will never be all rosy, nor will it always be gloomy. Ups and downs will both come. And after the high of the pups' birth, we were brought back down to reality in just one scary night.

In the privacy of her den Tina nursed her babies. The male, Denali, matched her color, tan with streaks of dark hairs. The female, Tonkawa, was black like Chinook. The three were dry and warm as the storm raged above ground. It never occurred to us that the den structure was unstable, or that the storm would produce torrential rain.

The next morning we were horrified by what we saw at the wolf exhibit—the entire area was flooded and the den was overflowing with mud. Frantically we started to dig. We prayed that somewhere in the collapsed mound we would find Tina and her pups alive. The deeper we dug, the deeper our feelings of desperation. When we were well beyond where her den should have been and didn't find them, we started to think maybe they hadn't been mired and trapped in the mud. Maybe Tina had moved her pups.

To our immense delight Tina proved herself a highly pragmatic, intelligent mother, and before the mud and rain sealed them underground she had carried

Tina crawls cautiously to the den entrance at night to eat.

Tina and her pups in the safety of their second den.

her pups to the safety of a secondary den site just twenty feet away. The alternate den had been man-made when the exhibit was built and was re-enforced with twelve-inch diameter pine logs and bolted together with steel rods. No amount of rain could wash it away.

Everyone felt a surge of puppy love. We were so happy Tina was such a bright and capable mother. We rejoiced in the survival of Tina and her babies, and I think the rest of the wolf pack was equally relieved.

Since Tina had worked so hard to save her pups we did not pull them when the fourteen day deadline arrived. They would stay with her and the pack.

Three weeks later while Tina lay next to me at the den entrance, and allowed me the honor of holding Tonkawa, I thought, *If only Shilo were here*. Or maybe she was. As I stared down at the pup I took solace that this tiny female's life would have a gentler, kinder path—new life, new hope, and not alone within the pack. 🐾

Tina, carrying Denali, and Chinook steer toward the man-made den.

Denali (male) and Tonkawa (female), born May 2, 1998.

Chapter 10

The Pack Divides

Though time helped to soften the pain of Shadow and Shilo's deaths, I never stopped feeling sad—I just felt the sadness less often. The wolves were my second family, and when enduring a family member's death, the sorrow is deep. Shadow and Shilo were my first. Their lives ended too soon, and with no help from me to prevent it. My heart is cemented in both guilt and grief, which remain to this day.

It seemed like a mere recess, but three years passed after Shilo died when there was talk of Heritage Zoo closing and its animals being dispersed. The news hit the citizens of Hall County hard and their loud criticism demonstrated what faithful zoo patrons they were. But in the end, none of their objections or their generous donations changed the outcome. Certain city officials wanted the zoo gone, and so it was.

Chinook and Tina's relationship was cut short. Chinook, his two offspring, and Solo were shipped to Wolf Haven International in Tenino, Washington, in January 2000. Yukon died before he could be relocated, and the other three were moved to Zoo Nebraska, 200 miles north of Grand Island because Wolf Haven did not have the space to take all the wolves. Dale and I accepted positions at Zoo Nebraska, allowing me to remain with Cheyenne, Montana, and Tina.

During the months that followed the split up, Tina, Montana, and Cheyenne adjusted to their new surroundings. For quite some time they seemed content to

Tina, Cheyenne, and Montana at Zoo Nebraska.

hold equal status rankings. But since a wolf pack does not function that way, eventually Tina reestablished herself as the alpha and Cheyenne the omega. And since Montana was the only male, he became Tina's alpha mate, a pairing he had wanted for years.

Since the fighting between Cheyenne and Tina never lessened, even after placing the three animals in a new zoo and a new exhibit, we were forced to put Cheyenne in a smaller independent area. It upset me to watch her pace along the fence line, wanting desperately to be with Montana and Tina—it reminded me of Shilo's fierce desire to be with her family when we had isolated her. She had constantly paced along the fence.

It was evident Cheyenne and Tina's lives would have to be spent peering at one another through wire mesh. Never again would they live together. After years of studying the wolves, I did not hesitate to separate them to keep them safe.

Because the three could not coexist in the same exhibit, we were back to square one. Cheyenne lived alone. Tina and Montana's pairing was manipulated by humans, but it was a bonding nonetheless. Cheyenne was denied even that. We had to rectify it.

Toward the end of the 1990s and into the next decade, facilities that kept gray wolves reevaluated how to house them. Far too many injuries and deaths of pack members brought this issue to the forefront. The Buffalo Zoo had a young wolf injured when the staff hurried the introduction of the adult animal to his pup. Visitors to the Brookfield Zoo witnessed five adult wolves viciously attack another pack member. The Folsom City Zoo's two sister wolves deposed their mother; she refused to submit to them and later died from her injuries sustained during the fight. And one of Cleveland Zoo's female wolves was attacked and killed by her pack.

It became apparent that trying to maintain a healthy pack of any size seemed unachievable. Therefore many captive wolf institutions made the decision to limit the number of animals within an exhibit to an individual pair. This has substantially reduced the fights and physical trauma to the wolves throughout facilities.

Once I learned of the widespread problem facing other zoos with regards to their wolves I was less harsh on myself. The news did not erase my sadness, but did remove some of my guilt.

Recognizing the importance of Cheyenne being paired up, we immediately began renovating the wolf exhibit and divided it into two distinct habitats. We contacted the same facility in Kalispell where we had obtained our original wolves in hopes they might have a male pup for us. He finally arrived in early June 2002. We named him Denali in honor of Tina's pup but also because the name means "high one," since he could jump incredible heights straight up in the air.

Throughout the summer of 2002, Denali was kept in a smaller exhibit north of the main wolf enclosure. He could see the others and they him. When they howled his ears perked up and he gravitated toward their voices. By late summer he was old enough to join Cheyenne. We walked him over to her exhibit, and the three adults ran to the fence. With their tails high and wagging, and their ears forward, all four wolves displayed an exhilaration that typifies wolf life when things are as they should be—harmonious.

The gates to Cheyenne's cage were opened, and Denali darted inside. He was too exuberant for her initially, since he was seven years younger, but once they exchanged body bumps, shouldered one another, and Cheyenne thoroughly smelled Denali, then the game of tag was on. She and that game had become synonymous. He ran and she followed; then she leapt up and put her front paws around his neck. He swung around, and acted out a gesture well known to dog owners—he dropped his front quarters into a crouch and with a wagging tail sprang at Cheyenne. This went on for about forty minutes over and over again. Tina and Montana celebrated the new introduction in their exhibit; the excitement was contagious. With their bodies sandwiched together, they trotted the outer edges of their cage and licked each other faces affectionately.

I beamed as the union unfolded. At last Cheyenne had a mate of her own. From then on, the wolves at Zoo Nebraska were known as the Elkhorn River Pack, named for a tributary of the river that flowed north of the zoo. 🐾

Second Denali, six weeks old, at Zoo Nebraska.

Epilogue

Since this story took place, the intervening years have been quite emotional for Dale and me. We left Zoo Nebraska and moved back to Canada in January 2005, leaving our wolf family behind.

Currently, Zoo Nebraska is under investigation by the U.S. Department of Agriculture for animal neglect and misconduct, because zoo personnel and several town locals shot and killed three chimpanzees when they escaped from their cages in September 2005. The zoo was forced to close its doors to the public in May 2007 and it will remain closed until USDA rules on their case.

As for the fate of Tina, Montana, Cheyenne, and Denali, only Tina and Montana were given a third chance at a good life. In spite of Wolf Haven kindly offering to take all four wolves, the truck to Tenino, Washington, carried only two crates holding Tina and Montana. The second trip scheduled for the following week, which would have transported Cheyenne and Denali, never occurred. Time ran out for them as it did for us, and we had no choice but to leave them behind at Zoo Nebraska. The same individuals who shot the chimpanzees also fired us and gave us three days to vacate the zoo house. Since we were not American citizens, we could not stay in the country. We returned to Canada leaving behind our home, our jobs, and all our beloved animals, including Cheyenne and Denali.

Sadly, Montana's life ended a mere two years later at Wolf Haven. He was euthanized in the winter of 2007, at the age of eleven, when his bone cancer became an unbeatable adversary. His life was cut short; captive wolves have been known to live well into their eighteenth year. People who knew Montana loved him and grieved with the news of his death. No doubt Tina felt the deepest loss; although they never produced pups together, their bond was strong, lasting seven years.

Happily Tina's loneliness would not last because she was introduced to a new mate, Nanook, who took an immediate interest in her. Tina had a quality that made her attractive to any male who knew her.

Chinook remains regal-looking with his prominent gray mask and is living out his life housed with his daughter Tonkawa at Wolf Haven.

Tina, Solo, and Cheyenne in their early days at Wolf Woods.

Shilo enjoying her bone.

In another enclosure at Wolf Haven, Solo still looks strong and striking but no longer dominates; Tina's pup Denali holds the alpha position while he and Solo spend their lives together.

As for me I cope with the reality of the pack's splintered lives by reflecting on the cherished moments each one of them bestowed on me. The memories are many: the first time Solo let me touch her. Watching Shadow amble over for his daily belly rubs. Tina offering me kisses and her pups. Staring into Shilo's eyes as she chewed a bone and shared her space. Montana spread eagle on the bottom of his wading pool, forever my baby boy. Chinook's enthusiastic greetings, and Cheyenne's passion for running and playing tag.

While life for the Heritage Pack was nothing if not challenging and unpredictable, I still treasure all the wonderful memories from my time with them.

Tina with Denali and Tonkawa.

Chinook greets the author with a kiss.

As for the wild wolves of Yellowstone, from the thirty original animals that made the park their home, new litters each year have now brought their numbers to approximately 300. They courageously forged a home for themselves in the wild land. They have proven they can survive.

Recent research indicates the Yellowstone wolves "appear to be boosting biological diversity around streams and helping nearly extinct stands of cottonwood trees to flourish again," reported *The Oregonian*. The presence of wolves has changed elk behavior causing them to "avoid high-risk areas such as stream beds," giving the young cottonwood and willow sprouts a chance to grow. The trees in turn "decrease erosion and add cooling shade over the stream," improving habitat for birds and fish.

Wolves have proven that they are essential in maintaining nature's balance. If for no other reason than to preserve our own future, wolves are valuable. An animal of mystery, they also spark human fascination. We are driven to learn more about them and to demystify their actions, their world. Hopefully we never learn so much about them that we ruin whatever it is that makes them so alluring. After all, it is their elusive presence as they silently cross through the forest, traveling the paths of their ancestors, stopping for a moment to sniff the air and listen, their piercing eyes glancing through the trees, then continuing on in search of survival that makes them a predator of such distinction. And if you are fortunate enough to walk in the tracks of the wolf, its spirit will forever guide you.

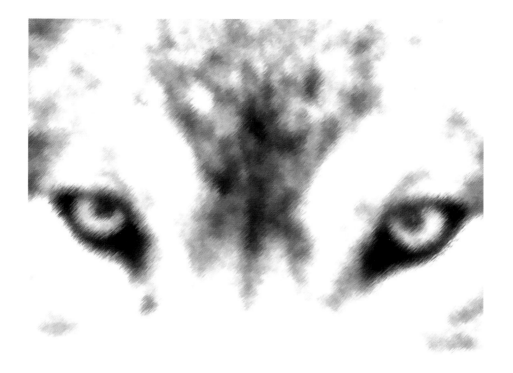

Reference Materials

Alderton, David. *Foxes, Wolves & Wild Dogs of the World*. New York: Facts on File, 1994.

Burton, John A. *Snakes: An Illustrated Guide*. London: New Burlington Books, 1991.

Busch, Robert H. *The Wolf Almanac*. New York: Lyons & Burford, 1995.

Croke, Vicki. *The Modern Ark*. New York: Scribner, 1997.

Dutcher, Jim, and Richard Ballantine. *The Sawtooth Wolves*. New York: Rufus Publications, 1996.

Fischer, Hank. *Wolf Wars*. Helena: Falcon Press Publishing Co., 1995.

Klinghammer, Erich, and Patricia A. Goodmann. *The Management & Socialization of Captive Wolves*. Battle Ground, IN: North American Wildlife Park Foundation, 1985.

Kundert, Verlag F. *Fascination*. Spreitenbach, Switzerland: F. Kundert, 1974.

Lopez, Barry Holstun. *Of Wolves and Men*. New York: Touchstone, 1995.

Mech, L. David, and Luigi Boitani. *Wolves Behavior, Ecology, and Conservation*. Chicago: The University of Chicago Press, 2003.

Millan, Cesar. *Cesar's Way*. New York: Harmony Books, 2006.

Montana Magazine, March 1999.

Ozoga, John J. *Whitetail Autumn*. Minocqua: Willow Creek Press, 1994.

Smith, Douglas W., and Gary Ferguson. *Decade of the Wolf*. Guilford: The Lyons Press, 2005.

Steinhart, Peter. *The Company of Wolves*. New York: Vintage Books, 1995.

Van Tighem, Kevin. *Bears*. Canmore, Alberta: Altitude Publishing Canada Ltd., 1997.

Warrick, Deborah M. "A Word on Flies," *Soul of the Wolf*. August 1996, 21-22.

Whitaker, John O, Jr. *The Audubon Society: Field Guide to North American Mammals*. New York: Alfred A. Knopf, Inc., 1980.

Whitt, Chris. *Wolves Life in the Pack*. New York: Barnes & Noble Publishing, 2003.

Wolf Reintroduction into Yellowstone. Member newsletter. Golden, CO: Call of the Wild Foundation, March 1995.

"Wolves Boost Biodiversity." In *Greenlines*, Vol. 31, 32-33. Animal Keepers' Forum: 2004. Originally published by The Endangered Species Coalition.

About the Author

Sandra Lynch-Bakken has been intrigued by nature most of her life, and for the past twenty years she has studied captive wolves. Growing up in Ontario, much of her spare time was spent photographing wildlife in Algonquin Park. When she and her husband moved to the United States in the early 1990s, she turned her lifelong passion into a career and became a wolf keeper. Sandra returned to Canada in 2005 and currently lives with her husband Dale on Vancouver Island where they both work for the SPCA. She is also working on her second book.